Environmental Management Systems

Environmental Management Systems

Understanding Organizational Drivers and Barriers

Stephen Tinsley and Ilona Pillai

London • Sterling, VA

First published by Earthscan in the UK and USA in 2006

ISBN-10: 1-85383-936-1
ISBN-13: 978-1-85383-936-8

Typesetting by Domex e-Data Pvt. Ltd, India
Printed and bound in the UK by Bath Press
Cover design by Yvonne Booth

For a full list of publications please contact:

Earthscan
8–12 Camden High Street
London, NW1 0JH, UK
Tel: +44 (0)20 7387 8558
Fax: +44 (0)20 7387 8998
Email: earthinfo@earthscan.co.uk
Web: **www.earthscan.co.uk**

22883 Quicksilver Drive, Sterling, VA 20166-2012, USA

Earthscan is an imprint of James and James (Science Publishers) Ltd and publishes in
association with the International Institute for Environment and Development

A catalogue record for this book is available from the British Library

Library of Congress Cataloging-in-Publication Data

Tinsley, Stephen, 1956-
Environmental management systems: Understanding organizational drivers and
barriers/Stephen Tinsley and Ilona Pillai.
P. cm.
Includes bibliographical references and index.

ISBN-13: 978-1-85383-936-8 (hardback)
ISBN-10: 1-85383-936-1 (hardback)

1. Industrial management – Environmental aspects. 2. Industries – Environmental
aspects. I. Pillai, Ilona. II. Title. HD30.255.T56 2005, 658.4'083011–dc22,
2005026231.

The paper used for the text pages of this book is FSC
certified. FSC (the Forest Stewardship Council) is an
international network to promote responsible
management of the world's forests.

Mixed Sources
Product group from well-managed
forests and other controlled sources
www.fsc.org Cert no. SGS-COC-2121
© 1996 Forest Stewardship Council

Contents

List of Boxes, Figures and Tables	*vii*
List of Acronyms and Abbreviations	*ix*
Preface	*xi*

1 The Theory of Environmental Management Systems

Introduction	1
Background	1
Environmental Risk Minimization	1
Organizational Drivers for Environmental Management	5
Interventions for Drivers	13
Economic Success Versus Environmental Improvements	13
Managing the Environment	14
Corporate Environmental Plan	14
The Development of Environmental Management Systems	15

2 Implementing an Environmental Management System

Introduction	25
Background	25
Management Commitment	26
The Environmental Audit	27
Aspects and Impacts Analysis	35
Register of Legislation	40
Objectives and Targets	43
Organization and Responsibility	44
Environmental Operating Procedures and Environmental Management Procedures	45
Monitoring and Measuring	56
Environmental Management System Audit	62
Management Review	68
The Corporate Environmental Plan	70
The Audit of Environmental Management Objectives, Policies and Activities	72
Environmental Management Plan Budget	72

3   Organizational Barriers

Introduction   77

Background   77

Organizational Theory   78

Organizational Barriers   78

Barriers in Small to Medium Enterprises   91

4   Models for Classifying Environmental Management Strategies

Introduction   93

Background   93

Types of Environmental Strategy   94

Studying Environmental Management Using Comparative Models   95

An Integrated Approach   104

Towards a Conceptual Research Model   109

5   Linking Environmental Management with Business Strategy

Introduction   113

Background   113

Devoid EMS Model   114

Isolated EMS Model   119

Devolved EMS Model   125

Integrated EMS Model   135

Use of Devoid, Isolated, Devolved and Integrated Models   146

Appendix: Examples of Environmental Charters   149

References   165

Index   *171*

List of Boxes, Figures and Tables

BOXES

1.1	Examples of corporate environmental disasters	2
1.2	Company initiatives that reduce environmental risk	5
1.3	Energy investment strategy	7
1.4	Example of cost savings made by waste minimization	8
1.5	Green company image at Volvo	9
1.6	Competitive advantage for Tetra Pak	9
1.7	Supply chain pressure	10
1.8	Examples of penalties for polluting	11
1.9	Greenhouse challenge plus	12
2.1	Template for audit report	67
2.2	Example of review meeting minutes	69

FIGURES

1.1	An environmental management system	18
2.1	Content of the environmental management plan	29
2.2	Control of nonconformities	46
2.3	Corrective action process	51
2.4	Document and data control	53
2.5	Impact opportunity or threat analysis	61
2.6	Environmental management procedure overview	63
3.1	Organizational barriers	79
4.1	Shelton's two paths for environmental management	105
4.2	A preliminary conceptual research model	110

TABLES

1.1	ISO 14000 standards	22
2.1	Aspects and impacts	36
2.2	Aspect classifications	37
2.3	Impact classifications	38
2.4	Probability of occurrence	39

2.5	Potential aspects and impacts probability matrix	39
2.6	Departmental aspects and impacts analysis matrix	41
2.7	Examples of objectives and targets format	42
2.8	Example of an audit questionnaire	66
3.1	Elements of an organization that can impact on the implementation of an EMS	78
3.2	Key managerial behaviours	82
3.3	Barriers for small to medium enterprises	91
4.1	Examples of typology models	96
4.2	Examples of continuum models	97
4.3	Main steps in a POEM system model	108
5.1	Devoid EMS model	114
5.2	Devoid profile of Company A	120
5.3	Isolated EMS model	121
5.4	Isolated profile of Company B	124
5.5	Devolved EMS model	125
5.6	Devolved profile of Company C	130
5.7	Devolved profile of Company D	135
5.8	Integrated EMS model	136
5.9	Integrated profile of Company E	141
5.10	Integrated profile of Company F	146

List of Acronyms and Abbreviations

BANC	British Association of Nature Conservationists
BATNEEC	best available techniques not entailing excessive cost
BCSD	Business Council for Sustainable Development
BSI	British Standards Institute
CAR	corrective action request
CBI	Confederation of British Industries
CERES	Coalition for Environmentally Responsible Economies
DEFRA	Department for the Environment, Food and Rural Affairs
DFE	design for the environment
DfES	Department for Education and Skills
EDF	environmental documentation folder
EHS	environmental health and safety
EMAS	Eco-management and Audit Scheme
EMP	environmental management procedure
EMS	environmental management system
ENDS	Environmental Data Services
EOP	environmental operating procedure
EPI	environmental performance indicators
ETNO	Environmental Charter of European Telecommunication Network Operators
EU	European Union
EUROPIA	European Petroleum Industry Association
EWG	environmental working group
FIDIC	International Federation of Consulting Engineers
H&S	health and safety
ICC	International Chamber of Commerce
IPPC	Integrated Pollution Prevention Control
JSA	Japanese Shipowners' Association
NCR	nonconformity report
NPI	new product introduction
OECS	Organization of Eastern Caribbean States
OEM	original equipment manufacturers
PCB	printed circuit board
PDCA	Plan-Do-Check-Act
PLF	plant load factor

POEM	product-oriented environmental management
R&D	research and development
SANPRoTA	Southern African Natural Products Trade Association
SBU	strategic business unit
SME	small to medium enterprise
TQEM	Total Quality Environmental Management
TQM	Total Quality Management
UKOTCF	UK Overseas Territories Conservation Forum
UNEP	United Nations Environment Programme
WBCSD	World Business Council for Sustainable Development
WEEE	Waste Electrical and Electronic Equipment
WICE	World Industry Council for the Environment
WRAP	Waste Reduction Always Pays

Preface

By addressing growing public concern for environmental sensitivity and the legislative requirements of industry, companies are gradually becoming more aware of the benefits of having an environmental focus. This has led to environmental management being viewed as an opportunity for companies to reduce their exposure to environmental risk. A company's environmental record affects its share price, its access to credit and its business credibility. It is this need for environmental credibility coupled with a company's increasing exposure to litigation that drives companies to manage environmental risk better.

An organization introducing an environmental management system (EMS) to meet its environmental needs should have an understanding of what those needs are. While environmental management will improve environmental performance, there are many other benefits depending on the proactive nature of the company and its willingness to increase its capacity in learning, innovation and environmental integration.

The various ways in which companies commit to environmental improvements suggest that there are different drivers for wanting environmental improvements and that the pursuit of these drivers varies from organization to organization. These drivers include energy efficiency, waste minimization, company image, competitive advantage, supply chain pressures, environmental legislative protection, staff morale and corporate social responsibility.

An EMS is a useful tool in ensuring that environmental improvements are met. The positive environmental impact of an EMS stems mainly from the fact that it is a systematic approach to environmental management. Implementing an EMS is a comprehensive exercise that must integrate environmental issues into every aspect of business management. The impact of environmental activities on corporate performance is strongly affected by the presence of a formal EMS. The ultimate aim of an EMS is to produce a corporate environmental plan, which will lead the company to improved environmental performance. However, monitoring and measuring the effectiveness of the EMS and therefore updating the corporate environmental plan regularly is key to a successful environmental improvement. An EMS entails: the use of audits, both internal and external; an understanding of the company's aspects and impacts; and objective-setting, culminating in a corporate environmental plan. If the company is to achieve continual environmental improvement, the environmental plan needs to be reviewed and examined regularly. The review should not be restrictive; it should encompass all aspects of the EMS.

However, many issues can arise when implementing an EMS and these can either facilitate or impede its implementation. From the existing environmental management and organizational theory literature, barriers to EMS have been found to include management style and commitment, and companies that succeed in achieving growth and innovation in environmental performance are often those that have managers who are good at empowering employees. Successful EMS implementation also relies on the integration of the EMS into existing business activities and management systems. Inappropriate planning to introduce an EMS into an organization is generally a risky strategy, while innovation can be the key to finding long-term successful solutions to environmental issues. In addition, those managers tasked with the responsibility of introducing EMSs often lack the necessary training and education, and companies that show trust in their employees to act responsibly have success in implementing a culture that demonstrates environmental improvement.

While an EMS provides a framework for implementing environmental improvements, the unique mixture of drivers and barriers within each company means that each must have their own environmental strategy, integrating business needs and environmental needs into realistic objectives and targets. An EMS offers a framework and accreditation system for organizations to use in creating continued environmental improvements. With different drivers towards EMS, however, the strategies adopted to achieve environmental improvement will differ so that no single strategy will suit every organization. For some companies, environmentalism is considered a threat and strategies are only implemented when required by environmental regulations. Other companies initiate voluntary transformation in environmental management to ensure continued improvement and competitive advantage.

In an attempt to improve understanding of environmental management, academics and practitioners have sought to classify corporate environmental behaviour and evaluate performance. This categorizing of characteristics helps one understand how drivers and barriers will shape environmental performance.

For example, those organizations in the process of implementation should have a lower environmental risk and reduced operational disadvantages. However, these companies are at risk when the implementation is stalled or they fail to achieve full accreditation. Lack of certification can mean that EMSs are not being monitored and verified, giving a company no security. In the worst case scenario, all the resources and efforts that have gone into implementing an EMS may be considered wasted if it cannot ensure compliance.

In another example, those companies with an accredited system that is only applied in isolation, and therefore separated from many of the daily operations of the organization, find a lack of communication and a lack of commitment from senior managers and directors as EMS is given a low priority against operational requirements. Environmental management models can therefore be used as a tool to assist decision-making in various areas of the business. This can be illustrated in the case of communication, which is a barrier identified in many of the model categories; management actions to overcome this barrier will vary according to the model the company follows. In addition, organizations may consider the implementation of a particular model to offer greater operational flexibility than their existing one.

In summary, an EMS linked to business strategy takes an organization beyond environmental risk management to offer options for customizing environmental systems to suit operational needs, market complexity and competitive strategy.

1

The Theory of Environmental Management Systems

INTRODUCTION

This chapter provides an introduction to the development of environmental management and to the organizational drivers that require managers to adopt environmental management systems (EMSs) to reduce the level of environmental risk to which their organizations may be exposed. This chapter also outlines some of the options available to reduce this risk.

BACKGROUND

It could be argued that public interest in the damage being caused by industry to the environment first began in the 1960s with the publication of Rachel Carson's *Silent Spring* (1962). Her book focused on the damage being done to the environment in Europe and North America by mass consumption and the intensive methods of farming and industrialization used to keep pace with consumer demand. She felt that the chemicals used in such intensive processes were poisoning the planet.

ENVIRONMENTAL RISK MINIMIZATION

Everything that consumers, companies, institutions and authorities do has a positive or negative impact upon the environment. The persistence of this view is fuelled by some managers believing that the pursuit of environmentally sound strategies is detrimental to the managerial goals of profitability, maintaining market share, cost control and production efficiency (Gallarotti, 1995). This view rests upon three fundamental assumptions. First, that management consider that the benefits of environmentally sound practices cannot be achieved because consumers are not prepared to pay the increased costs to industry. Second, the business costs of environmentally sound strategies are significant; and third, industry is not prepared to increase its investment in non-productive areas such as environmental risk aversion.

BOX 1.1 EXAMPLES OF CORPORATE ENVIRONMENTAL DISASTERS

Environmental disasters such as Three Mile Island and Exxon Valdez have drawn the public's attention to business activities and the effect they have on the environment.

Exxon Valdez

The supertanker Valdez, operated by US organization Exxon Group, ran aground in March 1989 on a reef in Prince William Sound, Alaska, due to human error. It spilled 11 million gallons of crude oil and caused one of the largest man-made ecological disasters. The oil slick covered 3000 square miles. While a clean-up plan outlined how an oil spill would be handled, including provisions for maintaining equipment (such as a containment boom) and a response team to be on 24 hour notice, a spill of this size had not been anticipated. To make matters worse, time was wasted as corporations, the Alaskan state government and the national government argued over who should take control of the situation, who would pay for what and who was responsible.

Three Mile Island

In 1979 a major nuclear incident occurred in America. A circulator pump failure inside a nuclear reactor, combined with a stuck pressurizer valve, allowed pressurized water coolant to escape. The reactor core overheated in minutes and core meltdown was narrowly avoided. As a result of mechanical and human error the total cost of clean up was in excess of US$1 billion. Changes that could have prevented this disaster, but which were only implemented afterwards, include:

- upgrading plant design and installing additional equipment to monitor radiation levels and mitigate accident conditions;
- installing an improved signalling system to avoid the confusion that hampered operations during the accident;
- regular analysis of plant performance by senior managers;
- enhancement of emergency procedures and preparations, including immediate notification of abnormal events and 24 hour staffing at monitoring sites.

Tokaimura

In September 1999 a nuclear power-related incident occurred in a uranium processing plant in Tokaimura, Japan. During the manufacturing process the enriched fissile fuel elements went critical when too much fissile fuel in the processing, coupled with the presence of water, caused further atoms to split, resulting in a momentary nuclear reaction. Radiation levels one mile from the site were reported to be about 15,000 times the norm. The incident registered 4–5 on the IAEA scale of 0–7 for nuclear incidents. The outcome of this 'error' was that 31,000 residents were affected, with 19 workers being hospitalized. Once again it was only after this accident that emergency plans, manuals, nuclear hazard prevention drills and lectures were provided, in an off-site emergency measures facility.

Chernobyl

In April 1986 a unit IV nuclear reactor at the Chernobyl nuclear power station in what was then the Soviet Union caught fire and exploded. Over 100 million curies of radiation were emitted with approximately half being deposited within 30 kilometres of the plant. Registering 5 on the IAEA nuclear incident scale, the cause of the incident was an experimental reduction in power from 3200MW to approximately 1000MW. During the experiment the reactor could not be stabilized quickly enough and power dropped to 30MW. Neutrons absorbing xenon in the core prevented the raising of the reactor power level to above 200MW. To counteract this, control rods were withdrawn resulting in the reactor becoming unstable and a slow nuclear chain reaction ensued that blew the top off the reactor. The subsequent fire was eventually controlled by dropping 5000 tonnes of boron, limestone and sand into the reactor from helicopters. Once again, the sheer magnitude of the disaster took everyone by surprise. Decisions that could have been carefully thought through beforehand were made as the disaster unfolded.

Lessons learnt

The aftermath of these disasters has seen major organizations suffer massive losses in terms of both finance and credibility. In addition, environmental legislation has grown quickly to reduce the risk of similar disasters occurring by making companies and their directors more responsible for any environmental neglect resulting from business activities. The most recent debates on the hole in the ozone layer and the cause of global warming have served to widen the public perception of what constitutes environmental impact. It is better understood that it is not just the car user, the multinational corporation, the government or the individual that is responsible but it is the responsibility of everyone to monitor and rectify environmental abuse.

Twenty years ago, there was virtually no debate over the relationship between environmental practices and corporate performance. It was taken as a fact that the organizational goals of economic development and the public demand for environmental protection were in direct opposition to each other. Thus the pursuit of environmental goals was a violation of the acceptable duty of managers to shareholders (Peattie, 1990; Prothero, 1990; Prothero and McDonagh, 1992;

Welford, 1996; Melnyk et al, 2003). The main objective of economic development is to maintain and gradually improve a standard of living for the existing population and for future generations (World Commission on Environmental Development, 1987). The main objective of environmental protection is to avoid, or limit, the problems with pollution, dereliction, loss of habitats and wildlife species arising from improved standards of living (Charter, 1992). Conflict arises when the cost of avoiding environmental damage is perceived as being a constraint on economic activity.

The strongly held tenets of traditional management thinking are continually being questioned and gradually being broken down (Melnyk et al, 2003). By addressing growing public concern for environmental sensitivity and the legislative requirements of industry, companies are gradually becoming more aware of the benefits of having an environmental focus. This has finally led to environmental management being viewed as an opportunity for companies to reduce their exposure to environmental risk. Managers have also begun to understand the corporate rewards of managing the environment, such as improved efficiency. Research has shown that there is profit in going green and that sound environmental management can lead to competitive advantage in business practice (Azzone et al, 1997; Banerjee, 2002). It has been predicted that the focus of companies will increasingly be on clean technology, competitive advantage, cost savings, environmental marketing, integrating environmental management into business functions and measuring environmental performance (Hale, 1995).

Many managers within industry still argue that some green issues are more relevant to other companies than to their own. They would also argue that environmental scientists and regulators have yet to agree among themselves on what constitutes being environmentally friendly (Kleiner, 1991). Therefore, despite mounting pressure on businesses to be environmentally aware, managers share no common understanding of what environmental awareness means within their own companies. However real or imagined these constraints, those companies who see regulations and government intervention as a constraint are jeopardizing their long-term future (Punjari and Wright, 1994).

In contrast, the pursuit of corporate environmentalism can be seen as a sound business strategy; managers who think environmentally increase profitability (Gallarotti, 1995). This view has been demonstrated in the past by the '3Ps' – 'Pollution Prevention Pays' devised by the company 3M, and by Dow Chemical's 'Waste Reduction Always Pays' (WRAP). A company's environmental record affects its share price, access to credit and its business credibility. It is this need for environmental credibility coupled with a company's increasing exposure to litigation that drives companies to better manage environmental risk. Companies are learning, through experience, that they cannot exist, much less prosper, without public acceptance (Buzzelli, 1991).

BOX 1.2 COMPANY INITIATIVES THAT REDUCE ENVIRONMENTAL RISK

3M

3M is a technology company with a worldwide presence in numerous markets: consumer and office; display and graphics; electro and communications; health care; industrial; safety, security and protection services; and transportation. 3M products include: Scotch® Tape, Post-it® Notes, medical/pharmaceuticals, abrasives and chemicals. In 1975 3M developed an environmental programme that aimed to eliminate pollution and save resources and money for the company. This was implemented through gaining a better understanding of product and process design and a commitment to quality improvements and innovation. The programme was named 'Pollution Prevention Pays' and was revised in 2002 to add new criteria, including a bigger drive for innovation and life-cycle analysis (Kotsmith, 2004).

Dow Chemical's 'Waste Reduction Always Pays'

In 1986 Dow formalized its waste reduction initiative, calling it 'Waste Reduction Always Pays', thereby integrating waste into Dow's pollution prevention code. As outlined by Castledine (2001), the WRAP programme had five basic goals:

1 continuous improvement in processes to reduce emissions and the volume of waste being treated;
2 recognition of employee efforts to motivate and encourage other employees to continue seeking new methods of waste reduction;
3 enhanced waste reduction mentality by having an employee-driven programme to promote waste reduction throughout the organization;
4 measuring progress to track waste reduction within each operating division;
5 reduced long-term costs through savings in fuel, raw material and environmental control costs.

ORGANIZATIONAL DRIVERS FOR ENVIRONMENTAL MANAGEMENT

An organization introducing an environmental management system to meet its environmental needs should have an understanding of what those needs are. However, not all organizations do understand their needs. If they did, there would be greater commitment to developing environmental management systems and commitment to the identification of the elements to be included in an EMS to ensure its success (Kirkland and Thompson, 1999). While environmental management will improve environmental performance, there are many other benefits depending on the proactivity of the company and its willingness to increase its capacity in learning, innovation and environmental integration. The various ways in which companies commit to environmental improvements suggest that there are different motivations for wanting environmental improvements (González-Benito and González-Benito, 2005).

More specific organizational drivers such as laws (regulations), lawsuits, government policies, banks, investors, accounting systems, employees, markets, costs, the public, environmental NGOs, industry codes and standards, self-regulation and international factors have been identified by Kirkland and Thompson (1999). They can be incorporated under seven main headings, each discussed in more detail below:

1   energy efficiency;
2   waste minimization;
3   green company image;
4   competitive advantage;
5   supply chain pressures;
6   environmental legislative protection;
7   staff morale and corporate social responsibility.

The pursuit of these drivers varies from organization to organization, to the extent that some organizations do not recognize the need for any environmental management (Walley and Whitehead, 1994).

Energy efficiency

This is the most logical starting point for those companies that wish to begin with something familiar that will provide a short-term return for minimum expenditure. A simple review of oil, electricity and gas bills will provide a base from which to measure future savings. Adopting an energy efficiency programme is a good way to begin an environmental awareness programme for the company. The corporate environmental policy would state that the organization is committed to using energy more efficiently. One of the key objectives might be to reduce energy consumption by 10 per cent in the first year, measured against existing energy bills.

Waste minimization

Many companies spend much of their business development budget on improving production or increasing sales. A greater return on investment, as high as 10 per cent of turnover, can be achieved if the same importance or investment

---

BOX 1.3 ENERGY INVESTMENT STRATEGY

Local authorities and local enterprise companies often provide free or heavily subsidized energy efficiency surveys for companies within their area. Using a mix of investment strategies can help resolve resources issues and achieve significant savings.

No investment

A simple programme of energy savings identification could begin with an examination of current electricity, gas, oil, water and effluent bills to ensure that the best possible prices are being achieved. A no investment strategy can realize significant savings by renegotiating rates with current energy suppliers or by changing suppliers. This strategy identifies immediate financial savings and educates organizations to the benefits of monitoring energy bills, even if it has no direct environmental benefit.

Low investment

A low investment strategy may involve the purchase of heating thermostats or optimizers to switch the heating on and off depending on external weather and seasonal conditions. Additional changes may include switching to slimline fluorescent tubes, which use approximately 8 per cent less electricity yet cost the same as standard fluorescent tubes. With a little more expense, compact fluorescent tubes use 75 per cent less electricity, last eight times longer and lead to an obvious reduction in replacement and maintenance costs.

High investment

Investing in a more efficient plant and equipment can involve significant capital expenditure and as a result can constitute a high investment strategy. New heating systems will be more efficient and if planned correctly, the initial capital expenditure will ensure future energy efficiency, low maintenance and eventual cost savings. They will also conform to the latest environmental legislative requirements.

---

is attached to improving waste management. Reducing waste improves profitability and any savings go straight to the bottom line and improve competitiveness. A waste minimization programme will improve business efficiency and reduce environmental impacts in the short term. Simple product or process design changes can result in fewer natural resources going into the final product. Waste should be seen as a product failure (Castledine, 2001; Ackroyd et al, 2003).

BOX 1.4 EXAMPLE OF COST SAVINGS MADE BY WASTE MINIMIZATION

Pioneer Technology UK Ltd manufacture set-top boxes, satellite decoders, DVD players and plasma televisions. As a result of the Producer Responsibility Legislation introduced in 1997, they started to identify opportunities for waste reduction. The company was spending UK£16,000 per year on waste disposal and began by using returnable, reusable and recyclable materials wherever possible. After four years it had reduced the waste spend to UK£4700 per year. The company involved the employees at all levels to ensure the new programme was successfully implemented. The company obtained ISO 14001 environmental certification in May 2000 and in preparation for the 2005 WEEE Directive (on Waste Electrical and Electronic Equipment) the company also undertook a solder recycling project resulting in a further UK£20 thousand per year saving (Pearson, 2004).

Green company image

Businesses strive continually to be different from their competitors and, in an attempt to gain a competitive advantage, products or services are often linked to environmental benefits. Many industry sectors are becoming increasingly aware that businesses and the general public prefer, where possible, to deal with companies that are able to demonstrate a willingness to operate in an environmentally responsible way (McBoyle, 1996). One example is Anita Roddick's Body Shop; Roddick saw at a very early stage the benefits to her company if it was perceived to be environmentally friendly. The Body Shop's green image went further by taking many environmentally sensitive stances, some of which were controversial. Customers thus believed that the company had sound ethics and it was perceived to be honest and forthright in all business matters.

Competitive advantage

If a company improves its efficiency in its use of resources, particularly in its production processes and use of energy and water, it will gain a competitive advantage over competitors that remain inefficient (González-Benito and González-Benito, 2005). Internally, efficient heating and lighting systems and safe handling of hazardous substances result in greater profitability, improved working conditions and a boost to staff morale, which may all, in a small less direct way, contribute to competitive advantage. Despite the fact that implementing an EMS programme is voluntary, using it as a means of pleasing customers is increasingly more common (Hui et al, 2001). While competitive advantage is one of the more elusive benefits of EMS

Box 1.5 Green company image at Volvo

Volvo was one of the first industrial manufacturing corporations in the world to adopt a formal environmental policy in 1972 and since then, Volvo has always stressed that environmental issues are fundamental to Volvo's future. The company is committed to full disclosure to their customers, employees and the public; internally the company communicates their environmental efforts by providing continuous environmental education courses for employees. The basis of this education is a formal training programme that extends to dealers, suppliers and contractors. Volvo also publishes an annual environmental report as a supplement to their annual report discussing environmental problems, goals, achievements and future plans.

Sweden has relatively strict environmental laws and high gas prices and taxes This has been an incentive for Volvo to develop fuel-efficient vehicles, alternative fuel vehicles and improve recycling. Environmental management systems are a key element to Volvo's environmental performance and so Volvo's EMS includes elements of ISO 14001 and the Eco-management and Audit Scheme (EMAS). Audits are conducted at regular intervals, by consultants or staff, to ensure that the environmental system is implemented (Kantz, 2000).

(Morrow and Rondinelli, 2002), some organizations actively seek environmental innovations and a competitive priority. These elusive competitive advantages will start to become more evident as more companies require ISO 14000 from their suppliers (Cochin, 1998). An example of this is part of 3M's 3P strategy (see Box 1.2) to eliminate pollution in the manufacture of its products (Azzone et al, 1997).

Box 1.6 Competitive advantage for Tetra Pak

Tetra Pak produces 100 billion aseptic cartons a year worldwide and controls 5 per cent of the market for liquid food packaging. In 2003, Tetra Pak launched their first national advertising campaign at a cost of UK£4 million. As Tetra Pak's customers are generally milk and fruit juice producers, it was not usual practice to directly aim advertising at the general public. However, the aim was strategically conceived to persuade the public of the environmental benefits of supplies in laminated paper-based cartons, thus giving Tetra Pak the competitive advantage of using a plastic alternative from a renewable source that can also be recycled. As Tetra Pak is no more expensive than the plastic alternatives, the company's marketing expenditure is well placed to ensure the company a profitable future (Caulkin, 2003).

Supply chain pressure

A study was undertaken by the Business For Social Responsibility Education Fund in 2001 to look at the growing pressure from supply chains to form environmental management strategies. Interviews with 25 suppliers suggested that a growing number of companies were seeking to address environmental issues across their supply chains. Distributors and dealers in the automotive sector faced the most requests for evidence of environmental strategy from manufacturers (González-Benito and González-Benito, 2005). In addition, a number of suppliers are involving their customers in changing product specifications to include pollution prevention activities.

Pressure along the supply chain may come in the form of suppliers having to have a fully accredited EMS or a more simple, yet still comprehensive, questionnaire requiring details of suppliers' environmental practices and performance (Ramus, 2002). Competitive advantage and supply chain pressure go hand-in-hand as customers demand that their suppliers meet their own environmental standard or lose their business. The competitive advantages of 'greening' a company will become more evident as more companies require ISO 14000 from their suppliers (Cochin, 1998).

Box 1.7 Supply chain pressure

Charter et al (2001) give examples of companies that expect environmental performance from their supply chain, some of which are described here.

Northumbrian Water

Northumbrian Water is a large water treatment and supply organization. The company has developed a strong EMS. There is a requirement for new contract suppliers to have or develop their own EMS. Environmental standards and performance now form part of the weighting for new tender contracts, managed through the supply chain department.

Lucent Technologies

The company has developed a life-cycle approach to products and services and analyses supplier performance in an integrated manner, taking into account price, delivery performance, service, quality and reliability, access to technology and environmental quality. To ensure that suppliers are aware of the commitments Lucent has made to the environment, the company has developed a list of banned substances for products and packaging, as well as guidelines for tracking and minimizing the use of environmentally hazardous substances. By sharing these requirements with suppliers Lucent has reduced all aspects of environmental impact in its products.

Environmental legislation

While managers may not pursue environmentally sound strategies using their own reasoning, they are being forced to by regulations (Azzone et al, 1997). Regulatory requirements are acknowledged as being the most important determinant of the number of staff a company will commit to environmental or health and safety issues (Khanna and Anton, 2002). The penalties for company transgressions have grown to incorporate significant fines and imprisonment for company directors. Those companies that have polluted in the past can no longer escape their clean-up responsibilities. The 'polluter pays' principle is central to existing environmental legislation and ensures that pollution caused by companies in the past is still their responsibility today.

The majority of environmental policy statements by large organizations declare that their objective is to improve environmental management and reduce exposure to environmental risk (British Standards Institute, 1992). The penalties for transgressing environmental legislative demands are high and are quickly becoming all encompassing (Ball and Bell, 1997). Despite these growing environmental pressures, however, most managers still hold to the notion that pollution pays and pollution prevention does not (Walley and Whitehead, 1994).

Environmental charters

A charter is a formal statement of the rights of an organization or a particular social group, which is agreed by or demanded from a ruling or a government. In the case of environmental charters, there are many companies, industries or governments that show their commitment to environmental issues by signing up to a charter. A wide range of charters is given as examples in the Appendix.

BOX 1.8 EXAMPLES OF PENALTIES FOR POLLUTING

The Environmental Data Services (ENDS) report records many cases of environmental pollution in the UK on a monthly basis. Recent examples include the following:

- A bio-diesel manufacturer was fined UK£17,000 after ignoring warnings that it was making too much noise by working outside permitted hours. Under the Integrated Pollution Prevention Control (IPPC) regime, the company pleaded guilty to four charges of operating outside permitted hours. The company's permit conditions were based on the fact that it had claimed that no significant noise could be detected beyond the bounds of the site and that they only planned to work between the hours of 8.00a.m. and 6.00p.m. While the company asked to have its working hours extended, they did not apply for this variation on their IPPC permit, as instructed (ENDS Report, 2005a).

- A foundry in the West Midlands was fined UK£45,000 for emissions of iron oxide. The company had breached conditions of their local authority air pollution control authorization, which prohibited 'persistent visible fumes'. The fumes had caused complaints from local people on several occasions (ENDS Report, 2005b).
- A waste carrier was fined UK£18,000 after transporting flammable solvent in an unsuitable tanker, causing it to leak across the site of the treatment works. The leakage occurred through the sight glass, which was made of acrylic plastic instead of glass. While the leakage occurred when the tanker was parked at the treatment site, it could have happened at any point throughout the tanker's journey and on trying to contain the spill, a worker got liquid on his hands and face (ENDS Report, 2005c).

Staff morale and corporate social responsibility

An indirect benefit of implementing an EMS is improved staff morale. While this is unlikely to be the primary driver for implementing an EMS in all but the most socially conscious businesses (González-Benito and González-Benito, 2005), it is becoming a greater priority with the advent of 'corporate social responsibility'. In the same way that a greener image can create greater customer satisfaction and loyalty, commitment to the environment can create job satisfaction and staff loyalty. While staff morale is not often directly measured as part of an EMS, anecdotal evidence is available (Morrow and Rondinelli, 2002; Hillary, 2004). Employees feel empowered to come up with their own solutions to improving the company's environmental performance, which results in the generation of new cost saving ideas (Cochin, 1998).

BOX 1.9 GREENHOUSE CHALLENGE PLUS

Greenhouse Challenge Plus is part of the Australian government's comprehensive Climate Change Strategy announced in 2004. The programme is managed by the Australian Greenhouse Office as part of the Federal Department of the Environment and Heritage.
  Greenhouse Challenge Plus aims to:

- reduce greenhouse gas emissions;
- accelerate the uptake of energy efficiency;
- integrate greenhouse issues into business decision-making;
- provide more consistent reporting of greenhouse gas emissions levels.

As part of the initiative, Greenhouse Challenge Plus has actively encouraged businesses to educate and motivate employees so that they change their workplace habits on a day-to-day basis. The Department of the Environment and Heritage states that one of the important indirect benefits of staff involvement in the initiative is that it boosts staff morale, which in turn contributes to higher productivity. It also acknowledges that the staff may have expertise that could contribute to a continuous improvement of greenhouse performance in the future, as well as creating environmental 'champions' within the workplace who could motivate others (Australian Department of the Environment and Heritage, 2005).

INTERVENTIONS FOR DRIVERS

In 2002, Khanna and Anton published a paper to determine if moves towards environmental improvements were based on the threat of regulatory penalties or the realization that environmental improvement offered opportunities for business improvement. They also looked at the types of intervention that would result depending on the perception of threat or opportunity.

Khanna and Anton categorized interventions into two types. Type I is internal management procedures such as policy development, audit operations and procedures, setting corporate standards, setting aside finances for liability costs and insurance, and appointment of environmentally aware staff. Type II is more external to the operations of the business and includes looking at the supply chain in greater depth and effectively getting suppliers, staff, customers and other stakeholders involved in improving environmental performance through training, publishing environmental reports and producing environmental policy statements.

The study concludes that threats such as regulatory requirements and inspections lead to the adoption of Type I interventions but have little likelihood of resulting in the adoption of Type II interventions. Opportunities such as closer contact with customers, greater chances of innovation and additional competitiveness lead to both Type I and II responses.

ECONOMIC SUCCESS VERSUS ENVIRONMENTAL IMPROVEMENTS

While the main objective of economic policy is to maintain and gradually improve a standard of living for the existing population and for future generations, the main objective of environmental policy is to avoid or limit the problems of pollution, dereliction and the loss of habitats and wildlife species arising from human activity. Short-term conflict can arise when the cost of avoiding environmental damage is perceived as being a constraint on economic activity, but with issues such as resource depletion and pollution becoming more prevalent, this conflict has to be overcome in the long term. In addition, due to a lack of environmental awareness and basic operational misunderstandings, managers often fail to identify whether environmental management is a functional or corporate activity. As a consequence, environmental management initiatives have floundered due to lack of company and management acceptance and commitment.

Despite assurances from bodies such as the Confederation of British Industries (CBI), the Department for Education and Skills (DfES) and the Department for the Environment, Food and Rural Affairs (DEFRA) in the UK, industry has been slow to accept the argument that there is profit in going green. Companies are being shown the advantages of environmental business opportunities by these bodies pursuing programmes of waste reduction, material reuse and recycling, and energy efficiency by introducing environmental management systems.

MANAGING THE ENVIRONMENT

Many managers and the general public are aware of the term environmental management but are unsure of its use, benefits or terminology. In a fast moving business environment managers do not get the time to learn new language and adopt new techniques. Environmental management is another form of management strategy to improve efficiency yet there is a lack of general knowledge to aid its introduction into organizations. One explanation for this may be a lack of environmental training, informative literature and knowledge within the ranks of middle and senior managers.

A study undertaken by Envirowise in 2000 and reported by Ackroyd et al (2003) demonstrates the lack of environmental awareness among businesses. Among UK businesses, 27 per cent did not know how to be more environmentally efficient, while 50 per cent of small to medium enterprises (SMEs) claimed they had no environmental impact.

All good business management textbooks will tell you that one of the functions of a manager is to provide stability to a company. Managers are tasked by their directors to ensure that a certain level of income and profitability is achieved with the minimum of corporate disruption. This philosophy does not apply to the environmental manager. The role of the environmental manager is to effect change. While other managers are managing stability, the environmental manager will be aware that the support of these managers when introducing environmental management and change will be needed.

CORPORATE ENVIRONMENTAL PLAN

As well as reducing corporate environmental risk, an environmental management plan can help to identify new business opportunities. As a communication tool the plan can be used to integrate all the environmental management activities of a company into one coordinated and easy-to-communicate action plan. Environmental management plans help managers to make explicit environmental management decisions within dynamic organizations, through a systematic process to achieve position, survival, growth and sustained competitive advantage within specified time horizons and acknowledged resource constraints.

A good environmental management plan will be useful for a number of reasons. It should:

- decrease environmental risk and lead to increased control over a company's future;
- provide direction and guidelines for the introduction of new products;
- identify the benefits of new design changes to existing products and processes;
- contain enough detail of a company's environmental management objectives, activities and direction to allow the day-to-day implementation of environmental management activities to be carried out by junior employees or managers;
- provide all staff with a better understanding of environmental management activities and the importance of environmental management to the development of the company;
- encourage company identity and team spirit, increasing the motivation of both environmental management and non-environmental management staff associated with the planning process;
- keep ahead of competitors.

THE DEVELOPMENT OF ENVIRONMENTAL MANAGEMENT SYSTEMS

The introduction of environmental legislation and regulation stimulated companies to seek ways to minimize their exposure to environmental risk. The introduction of a system integral to business activities seemed to be the most effective way of managing and minimizing environmental risk, minimizing resource use and allocating responsibility for achieving results (Hui et al, 2001; González-Benito and González-Benito, 2005).

An EMS has been defined by the British Standards Institute (1992) as 'The organizational structure, responsibilities, practices, procedures and resources for determining and implementing environmental policy'.

Safety audit

Many organizations, in response to growing environmental pressures, adopt EMSs and conduct environmental audits to reduce the level of environmental risk (Welford and Gouldson, 1993). The first attempt at addressing these environmental concerns was the safety audit (Local Government Management Board, 1991). It was accepted, particularly in the oil and petrochemical industries, that production processes can go wrong and employees are occasionally injured, hence it seemed natural for companies in these industries to extend their sphere of concern from the local community to the local environment (Wheeler, 1993). While the safety audit may have been a logical place to begin, it was very much ineffectual as an environmental strategy because practices and standards varied from country to country (Wheeler, 1993).

Total Quality Environmental Management

The second attempt at environmental control was to treat environmentalism as a 'quality issue' and introduce measurable standards such as Total Quality Environmental Management (TQEM) and BS 7750 (British Standards Institute, 1992). These functions of quality measurement were seen as extensions of existing Total Quality Management (TQM), BS 5750 and ISO 9000 standards and carried low priority status, particularly against daily operational requirements (Tinsley and Melton, 1997).

However, the steady increase in environmental legislation and the increasing cost of corporate administration and compliance are the major drivers in moving companies beyond pollution control and to see future environmental investment as a method of reducing compliance costs.

Those companies with existing TQM systems saw the benefits of decreasing manufacturing costs, achieving faster time to market and the increased market share that would follow by introducing environmental management systems. However, while some companies were achieving success with environmental management strategies, others found their strategies had to be shelved or abandoned altogether (Shelton, 1994). The main reasons for such actions were a lack of support for the environmental management system by middle managers, lack of commitment by senior management, and inability to communicate the benefits of further environmental investment. Due to the increasing severity of penalties for environmental management failure, large organizations this began to adopt EMSs that focus on the 'management' of environmental risk.

Eco-management audit

The third phase of EMS development was the environmental audit. This led to the creation of 'eco-management audit' frameworks such as BS 7750 and ISO14001 and EMAS (Eco-Management and Audit Scheme), which were designed for national and international standards (British Standards Institute, 1992; Commission of the European Communities, 1993; ICC, 1994). ISO 14001 eventually superseded BS 7750 and is applicable to all companies worldwide, whereas EMAS applies only to industrial companies and some public sector organizations, and only European Union (EU) member states can participate (Welford, 1996).

The role of the environmental audit was to be a process of checks and balances that formed part of a virtuous circle of improvement for the environmental management system (Elkington and Hailes, 1987). It was argued that audits would lead to the identification of risks as well as pinpointing cost saving opportunities. However, due to the pressures brought to bear in complying with legislation, too many companies used audits solely to verify and achieve compliance (Welford, 1996).

Environmental management systems

Finally the environmental management system itself was devised. Emphasis was placed on 'management' to control policy issues, internal resources, purchasing, product or service design, communication and education. Such emphasis was designed to allow the measurement of management decision making and environmental consequences and to make environmental management part of daily operational activity.

Although national and international bodies are setting standards for levelling the business playing field, it still remains true that for many companies environmentalism is merely about compliance (Avila and Whitehead, 1993). This view is shared by Shrivastava and Hart (1994), who argue that a 'command and control' style regulation, which forces companies to approach environmental issues in a fragmented fashion, has produced little progress.

Figure 1.1 identifies the type of system that would be required to implement an effective EMS into an organization (Welford and Gouldson, 1993). The system, based on a TQM structure, is designed to ensure that environmental management is up to a 'quality' standard. The reasoning for such strategic configuration is that similarities between 'quality' systems and environmental management systems provide management with familiar reference points (Welford, 1996). Conflict can occur, however, if both systems are in opposition and resources and management are divided as to the best option to take (Tinsley and Melton, 1997).

Similarly, each system may vary between organizations depending on their structure and the level of environmental commitment by senior management. The more complex the EMS, the more organizational forces will act against, rather than for, its successful acceptance into an organization (Roome, 1992).

As some organizational change is required with the implementation of any strategic change it is worthwhile noting that the more radical the shift, the more resistance will be encountered. More resources will be needed to overcome the resistance and more uncertainty will be introduced into the organization (Roome, 1992). In short, the more intricate the strategy, the greater the organizational

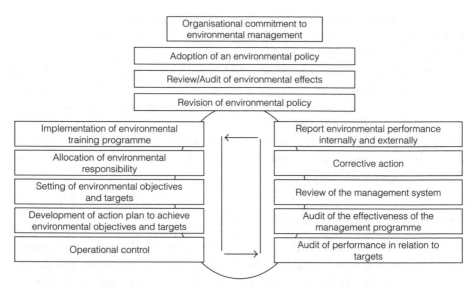

Figure 1.1   *An environmental management system*

Source: Welford (1996)

barriers that will block its successful acceptance. With the introduction of any new strategy, there will always be company forces acting for and against its introduction.

Those companies with existing TQM systems saw the benefits of decreasing manufacturing costs, improve delivery time to market and increased market share that resulted from the introduction of EMSs (Shelton, 1994). However, Shelton's study found that, while some companies had successful EMSs, others soon abandoned theirs. One reason appeared to be that companies 'hit the green wall' of a lack of support for the environmental management strategy concept, lack of environmental strategy focus, and the inability to communicate the benefits of further environmental investment.

The existing dilemma for senior management is that they are advised that good environmental management is rewarded with reduced operational costs, improved value of a product, operational efficiency, new marketing outlets, enhanced corporate image and new business opportunities (Taylor, 1992; Hui et al, 2001). It is also advised that environmental management could be the next strategic management tool for competitive advantage (Greeno and Robinson, 1992). A dilemma arises,   however, because this advice is contrary to management's awareness of the business reality that an EMS is just another newly emerging corporate strategy that must be given the time and resources to be accepted as part of the existing corporate culture (Rothenberg, Maxwell and Marcus, 1992).

Environmental academics and practitioners are aware that organizations are spread along an environmental continuum with 'beginners' and 'proactivists' at opposing poles (Hunt and Auster, 1990). Some of the main reasons for the varying levels of environmental commitment are stated as availability of resources and the commitment of senior management (Greeno and Robinson, 1992; McGrew, 1990). However, the commitment of resources and senior management according to Roome (1992) will not, in itself, ensure the successful introduction of an EMS. An effective EMS, he adds, must promote quality and commitment, by an organization and its employees, to an environmental ethic.

In implementing environmental management systems, Hunt and Auster (1990) point to the benefits of a phased installation process. They suggest that organizations adopt a phased approach to introducing EMSs depending on the available resources and the commitment of senior management. EMSs such as BS 7750 and ISO 14001 are designed to help organizations develop a formalized management process (Hui et al, 2001).

This history of the development of environmental management systems provides an insight into the road that has been travelled and the experiences learned along the way by others. The majority of large companies have environmental management systems and environmental policy statements declaring that their objective is to improve environmental management and reduce exposure to environmental risk.

To address the issue of environmental performance in industry, environmental standards were considered to be the best way to demonstrate the benefits of better environmental management to industry and to offer a process, similar to the familiar BS 5750 quality assurance standard, to reduce the risk of exposure to the increasing numbers of European environmental directives.

BS 7750

BS 7750 was the first UK national standard created for an environmental management system in the 1990s (Morrow and Rondinelli, 2002). Based on the BS 5750 quality system, the BS 7750 was used to describe a company's EMS, evaluate its performance and to define policy, practices, objectives and targets, and to provide a catalyst for continuous improvement.

The concept is similar to that used in quality standard BS 5750 and the superseding ISO 9000, in that the methods are open to definition by the company. The standard provides the framework for development and assessment of the BS 7750 environmental management system. BS 7750 was developed as a response to concerns about environmental risks and damage (both real and potential). Compliance with the standard is voluntary and complements the requirements for compliance to statutory legislation. As BS 5750 was the driver for ISO 9001, so BS 7750 led to the development of ISO 14001. BS 5750 and ISO 9000 do not relate to quality in environmental terms but there are many similarities both in terms of management implications and also the registration process (Ball, 2002).

Fundamentally, BS 7750 requires the environmental policy to be fully supported by senior management; policies must be outlined to both staff and the general public. The policy needs to clarify compliance with environmental legislation that may affect the company and it must stress a commitment to continuous improvement. Emphasis is placed on policy as this provides the direction for the remainder of the management system.

The preparatory review and definition of the organization's environmental effects is not part of a BS 7750 assessment but examination of these data will provide an external auditor with a wealth of information on the methods adopted by the company. The preparatory review itself should be comprehensive in its consideration of input processes and output at the site. It should also be designed to identify all relevant environmental aspects that may arise from the company works. These may relate to current or future operations, as well as to the activities performed on site in the past (such as contamination of land).

EMAS

The Eco-Management and Audit Scheme is similar in structure to ISO 14001 and was launched in 1995. There are two major differences between EMAS and ISO 14001. First, the whole company can be certified to ISO 14001 whereas EMAS is generally a site-based registration system. Second, whereas any company from any business sector can use ISO 14001, EMAS is only available to those companies operating in the industrial sector.

Within the UK, an extension to EMAS has been agreed for local government operations, which may also register their environmental management systems to the EMAS regulations. In addition to a summary of the process, the statement requires quantifiable data on current emissions from the site and environmental effects, the amount and types of waste generated, raw materials utilized, energy and water resources consumed, and any other environmental aspect that may relate to operations on the site.

Pre-assessment is as much part of EMAS as it is of ISO 14001. The environmental audit must be comprehensive in its consideration of input processes and output at the site. The procedure is designed to enable identification of all relevant environmental aspects that may arise from the site itself. The pre-assessment will also include a wide-ranging consideration of the legislation that may affect the site, whether it is being complied with currently, and perhaps even whether copies of the legislation are available. Many of the environmental assessments undertaken have already highlighted the fact that companies are unaware of all the environmental legislation that affects them, and therefore fail to meet the requirements of that legislation.

Under the EMAS standard the company declares its primary environmental objectives as those that have the greatest environmental impact. In order to gain most benefit, these objectives become the primary areas of consideration within both the improvement process and the company's environmental programme. The programme will be the plan used to achieve specific goals or targets and describe the real and achievable means to be used to fulfil those objectives.

As with ISO 14001, the EMAS standard requires a planned, comprehensive and periodic series of audits of the EMS to ensure that it is effective in operation, is meeting specified goals and continues to perform in accordance with relevant regulations and standards. The audits are designed to provide operational information in order to exercise effective management of the system, providing information on practices that differ from current procedures or offer an opportunity for improvement. Under EMAS the bare minimum frequency for an audit is every three years.

Most companies are used to producing an annual report and accounts describing the activities of the organization over the previous year and their plans for the future. EMAS generally requires a similar system for the company's environmental performance. It is also requires that there should be notice of any particular plans for the future that may have an effect upon the environmental performance of the organization, whether detrimental or beneficial.

The peculiarity with EMAS is that the policy statement, programme, management system and audit cycles are reviewed and validated by an external, accredited, company. In addition to providing a registration service, this company is also required to confirm, and perhaps even sign, the company's periodic environmental statements.

Environmental management system standardization: ISO 14001

At the same time as the European Commission put forward a proposal for EMAS, the British Standards Institute (BSI) in the UK also devised an environmental assessment standard called BS 7750. It was based on the quality standard BS 5750 and was launched after consultation with industry and a two-year pilot programme. The objective of BS 7750 was to put the emphasis on the management of environmental systems, not just the systems themselves.

The BS 7750 and EMAS standards were very similar in environmental requirements for businesses. At the time it was thought appropriate to make EMAS a mandatory standard for businesses. Strong industry lobby groups argued successfully, however, that a mandatory approach would be detrimental to industry and EMAS is now a voluntary scheme.

In 1993 it was felt that an international standard was required for environmental management. In 1996, from an idea based on BS 7750, the ISO 14001 standard was born (Morrow and Rondinelli, 2002). It was argued to be a step forward given the successes of the quality standard ISO 9000 and intended to replace the numerous and often conflicting sets of criteria found in various countries. ISO 14001 focuses on the processes involved in the creation,

Table 1.1 *ISO 14000 standards*

Standard	Description
14000	Guide to environmental management principles, systems and supporting techniques
14001	Environmental management systems – Specification with guidance for use
14010	Guidelines for environmental auditing – General principles of environmental auditing
14011	Guidelines for environmental auditing – Audit Procedures - Part 1: Auditing of EMSs
14012	Guidelines for environmental auditing Qualification criteria for environmental auditors
14013/15	Guidelines for environmental auditing – Audit programmes, reviews and assessments
14020/23	Environmental labelling
14024	Environmental labelling – Practitioner programmes – Guiding principles, practices and certification Procedures of multiple criteria programmes
14031/32	Guidelines on environmental performance Evaluation
14040/43	Life cycle assessment – General principles and practices
14050	Glossary
14060	Guide for the inclusion of environmental aspects in product standards

management and elimination of pollution, rather than solely on directly reducing pollution (Melnyk et al, 2003).

As BS 5750 had been withdrawn with the appearance of the ISO 9000 series, the outcome of the emergence of the international standard ISO 14001 meant that the national standard BS 7750 together with national standards in other EU countries were, with common consent, also withdrawn. Since the introduction of ISO 14001 many other ISO 14000 standards have also come into operation; the list is shown in Table 1.1.

The ISO 14001 standard is a process, not performance standard, that describes a system to help an organization achieve its own environmental objectives. It is assumed that by helping a firm focus on its manufacturing process, the firm will improve its environmental performance (Melnyk et al, 2003).

BS 8555/ Project Acorn
The most recent development designed to assist all sizes of business to achieve ISO 14001 is the phased EMS implementation approach used by BS 8555 and

piloted through Project Acorn. This method focuses on introducing greater flexibility to achieve the ISO 14001 standard by breaking the process down into bite-size pieces. It provides a six-level staged approach as follows:

1   A commitment to the ISO 14001 standard and establishing of a baseline through which to monitor continuous improvement.
2   Compliance with customer needs and legal and regulatory requirements.
3   Identification of significant environmental aspects and impacts for the development of objectives and targets and the management programme.
4   Management of significant environmental aspects using the management programme.
5   Documentation check, audit and review of the environmental management system.
6   External communication to gain full accreditation against an internationally accepted EMS standard.

After each phase of the scheme has been implemented, the organization can either assess itself through internal audits, allow major customers to assess it or be assessed by a third party, to ensure that the requirements of each phase have been met (Acorn Trust, 2005). Undergoing an external audit may have added benefits to both customers and suppliers because the evidence may be used to avoid second party audits of their supply chain (Gascoigne, 2002).

In some cases organizations may not necessarily have to achieve full certification before becoming part of a major supply chain. Achieving level three of BS 8555 is often enough to be accepted as a supplier. However, more and more companies are looking for international accreditation to acknowledge their environmental commitment (Khanna and Anton, 2002).

In Chapter 2, the implementation of environmental management systems is discussed, including an overview of the main stages, such as audits and impact and aspects analysis, as well as some practical templates that may be used to structure individual procedures.

2
Implementing an Environmental Management System

INTRODUCTION

The positive environmental impact of EMS stems mainly from the fact that a systematic and comprehensive approach to environmental management leads to the discovery and exploitation of new 'win–win' potential (Steger, 2000). In this chapter the basic frameworks of EMSs are discussed. This includes a discussion of audits, impact and aspects assessments, keeping abreast of legislative requirements, the resource commitment required and the mechanisms needed to ensure continuous improvement.

BACKGROUND

The roots of EMS can be traced to the mid-1980s when companies strove to comply with increasing stringent environmental legislation in the US. At the same time, innovative companies in Europe were developing a more proactive attitude towards environmental issues, viewing them as a business opportunity. In a search for managerial toolkits that would aid the implementation of environmental strategy, environmental audits first began being used as risk management tools that would later form the basis of environmental management systems (Steger, 2000).

An EMS is a transparent, systematic process with the purpose of implementing environmental goals, policies and responsibilities, and mechanisms for auditing these elements (Steger, 2000). Implementing an EMS is a comprehensive exercise that must integrate environmental issues into every aspect of business management. To achieve quality a company must gain control of every aspect of the business, including any environmental implications. According to Hale (1995), control is gained by:

- finding out what needs to be controlled;
- deciding how to control it;
- implementing a system of control;
- maintaining control.

Implementing an EMS not only ensures that all four aspects of control are gained, it also ensures that environmental issues are given due consideration along with finance and product quality. An EMS usually has a positive impact on a company's bottom line by providing the mechanism for continued improvement for resource efficiency, customer needs and ultimately financial performance. The impact of environmental activities on corporate performance has been shown to be strongly affected by the presence of a formal EMS. The improvement generated by the presence of a certified EMS can be explained by the way it involves people in the environmental activities of their company. Alternatively, the evaluation by an impartial third party may motivate improvements. It could also be argued that benefits are generated from focusing on underlying processes resulting in long-term improvements in levels of pollution and in operations performance (Melnyk et al, 2003).

The components of an EMS management plan are summarized in Figure 2.1 and each aspect is discussed in further detail below. EMSs such as ISO 14001 are based on Deming's Plan-Do-Check-Act (PDCA) management cycle (Ammenberg and Sundin, 2005). The ultimate aim of an EMS is to produce a corporate environmental plan that will lead the company to improved environmental performance. However, this chapter argues that monitoring and measuring the effectiveness of the EMS and therefore regularly updating the corporate environmental plan is key to successful environmental improvement.

MANAGEMENT COMMITMENT

To ensure the successful installation of an environmental management system it is essential to engage full management commitment. People and budgets must be made available, together with the dedication of one or more of the senior management team to the project. If possible, at least one director should be recruited on to the working group. Lack of support from above will make the implementation process difficult, if not impossible. There will be many political issues to overcome throughout the implementation process and more efficient headway will be made if a director handles the political negotiations.

Environmental policy statement

Within the scope of the company activities, products and services, senior management commitment should include a signed environmental policy statement, setting out the commitment to protect the environment, prevent pollution and continuously improve company environmental performance. It forms the backbone on which the EMS hangs and indicates to internal and external stakeholders that the company is serious about protecting the environment (Ramus, 2002). An example of the plan's aims could include energy and water consumption, reducing waste generation and reducing emissions.

The plan should also state what the company will do to meet the stated aims, perhaps identifying some of the following:

- Provision of adequate resources and personnel to maintain the EMS.
- Measures to ensure employees are educated and trained to understand their responsibilities in respect of the environmental policy.
- Measures to ensure that the requirements of environmental legislation are met and where possible, exceeded.
- Provision of a framework for setting environmental objectives and targets.
- Integration of environmental considerations into the design of products and services in order to avoid or minimize environmental impacts.
- Systems to monitor environmental performance continuously.
- Revision and audits of the effectiveness of the company environmental policy.
- Work to improve the environmental performance of suppliers, contractors and subcontractors where feasible.

The statement should be signed and dated by the managing director, other director or senior manager to demonstrate senior management support for the initiative.

THE ENVIRONMENTAL AUDIT

The environmental audit requires an analysis of the current level of environmental risk and where the company stands in relation to it. The audit is a prelude to determining the future objectives of the company and the procedures for achieving these objectives. It is a process of extracting information about the company that, when analysed, will provide a realistic assessment of how the company affects the environment, plus a set of environmental objectives and targets to reduce those effects. The establishment of the objectives and targets will form the basis of the corporate environmental plan.

An environmental management audit is often lengthy, with the implications summarized as part of an aspects and impacts analysis. Therefore, an environmental management audit is not usually included as part of the environmental management plan, presentation or report. If it is required in the report, it should be included as an appendix at the end of the plan.

Any environmental management audit includes an analysis of both external and internal factors. External factors may arise from the environment, customers and/or competition. They relate to circumstances that the company cannot control directly and include broad factors such as the economy, customers, competitors and operational policy.

The need for auditing

Most people in business have their own impression of what constitutes an audit. The audit process for an environmental management system has two parts. First, the pre-environmental management system audit will provide knowledge of what the business activities are and what impact they have on the environment (internal audit), as well as those forces outside the business that may not be easily controlled (external audit). Some of these activities will have a positive or negative impact upon the environment. The information gained from this audit will provide evidence for the chosen environmental management objectives and targets. Second, the EMS audit is designed to ensure that the environmental management system and its associated procedures are in place and actually work. This second part therefore only occurs once the EMS has been implemented and sufficient time should be given for the EMS and its procedures to function before this final audit is undertaken. Implementing ISO 14001 requires that the environmental management systems operate for a minimum period of three months before final auditing.

Internal audit

An internal environmental audit is undertaken to assess what products and services the company currently produces. It also assesses the impact operational activities have upon the environment. From this audit a list of operating aspects that have an impact upon the environment can be created. An internal audit allows management to determine the level of impact each aspect has and how significant it is to the company's operations. The results of this internal analysis will be used to form the basis of the aspects and impacts analysis, as explained below.

Factors in an internal appraisal

When identifying the most relevant areas and activities in the company to appraise, use of discretion and judgement is needed to select areas to appraise because the most relevant internal factors will vary between industries, companies and individual departments. A useful starting point is to list the major areas of company and departmental activities and the resources that are critical to competitive success. Essentially these are those activities and resources that result in outputs valued by existing customers, indeed it may be useful to ask customers' views as an aid in the identification process.

A checklist of some of the factors and areas likely to form the internal part of the environmental management audit include:

- Finance:
    - liquidity;
    - profit margins.

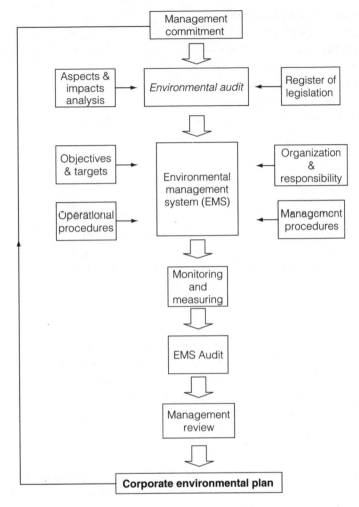

Figure 2.1   *Content of the environmental management plan*

- Personnel:
  - managerial experience and expertise;
  - levels of training and education;
  - motivation and attitudes;
  - workforce skills.
- Research and development and design:
  - budgets;
  - innovative success;
  - design expertise;
  - technological expertise.
- Engineering and production:
  - production planning and control systems;
  - degree of automation;

- quality control procedures;
- age profile of plant;
- flexibility;
- unit costs of production;
- supply and procurement.
- Environmental management:
  - environmental research and information systems;
  - environmental planning systems;
  - staff attitudes;
  - company image.

Finance

While checking the overall finance of the company as part of the internal audit, it is prudent to establish the likely cost of implementing the EMS, as it will vary from company to company and across industry sectors. The cost of implementing an EMS in relative terms should not be high.

Personnel

Taking the time to identify the gaps in training, motivation, skills and so forth, and establishing development programmes will aid swifter implementation. Use existing quality, health and safety or similar training structures to which environmental training can be added effectively. This will save on company resources and minimize operational disruption.

Research and development and design

When using research and development (R&D) and design capability, consider the potential results of environmental changes to existing products and services. Consider whether some environmental changes will allow the company the opportunity to offer better products to the market, or will a new or modified process offer additional savings or by-product. Many by-products have emerged from companies looking at alternative uses for their product or process waste.

Engineering and production

Focusing on the engineering and production activities of the company may identify current and future challenges or present new opportunities. Consider, for example, some of the following areas for investigation:

- technology – materials, components and machines;
- techniques – methods, systems;
- design, promotion, presentation;
- changes in legislation.

Closer inspection of existing methods of operation and the identification of alternative uses or changes to the production processes or engineering methods can bring significant benefits to material usage and energy efficiency.

Environmental management

During the auditing process it is useful to take the time to check for the existence of environmental management skills and experience. Identifying those employees with relevant environmental skills will help when recruiting for the working group.

Techniques of environmental assessment

Information pertaining to finances and the running of day-to-day operations should all be available through company records, however, employee interviews, focus groups (discussion groups) and questionnaires are three of the more common and easier methods of gathering additional information for an audit.

Employee interviews

Depending on the size of the company, all employees or a cross-section can be interviewed. If it is to be a cross-section ensure that every employee level and department is represented. This will gather a range of views and ideas for environmental improvement. The interviews can be either structured, seeking answers to specific operational questions, or unstructured, whereby just a few open-ended questions are asked and the employees express their views across a broad spectrum of subjects relating to the question.

Focus groups

Formed from a representative cross-section of the company, a focus group discusses the subject of environmental issues within the company. Notes are made of agreement and areas of discussion that come from the group. The size of the group may vary with the size of the company but the optimum size of focus group is considered to be 8–12 members (Eisenhardt, 1989).

Employee survey

A simple one page survey or questionnaire with a few questions about operations and environmental impact can be very effective and easy to administer. A simpler option, but one that can have just as much benefit, is a memo asking everyone in the company what environmental improvements they would like to see introduced. The memo approach is less structured and will elicit all kinds of responses from employees, some relating to the environment, to some health and safety and some even raising the odd grievance. The environmental suggestions received will form the basis of the company's environmental objectives and targets.

The use of surveys in the environmental management audit can ensure a systematic approach is employed and at the same time help guarantee that individual process or product managers are not, for example, avoiding aspects of environmental responsibility that may show them in a poor light.

External audit

The external environment encompasses all of the forces and factors outside a business that have some impact on it but that it cannot influence or control. The first problem is to identify the key factors pertinent to a particular department or unit and, where appropriate, the business. In this phase the environmental issues that currently have or will have an impact on the business should be considered.

The biggest issue for most companies at present is the growth in environmental legislation that has, or should have, an immediate impact on a company's operational policy and decision-making process. However, in broad terms it is possible to identify distinct groups of environmental factors, which, to a greater or lesser degree, potentially affect all industries and organizations. These include the influence of environmental pressure groups, which can draw negative publicity to a company not seen to take the environment seriously. More importantly, there is also influence from consumers who are becoming more educated in environmental matters. Additionally there are competitors who may have strategies for environmental performance that give them a competitive edge. All of these factors should be listed as potential environmental pressures during an external audit.

Environmental pressure groups

Although these groups may apply pressure in different ways they are all very strong in the lobbying arena. They are not afraid to take on the largest of companies and they are adept at coming out on top in media battles. An example of this would include the media exchange between Shell and Greenpeace on the scrapping of the Brent Spar oil rig in 1998. It was arguably a disastrous public relations exercise for Shell and the proposed dumping of the Brent Spar at sea was abandoned in favour of the public demand for a Greenpeace-initiated land-based disassembly. Multinational companies increasingly look to create working partnerships with environmental groups and seek environmental input from them before actions are taken. Examples of environmental pressure groups include:

- Friends of the Earth;
- Greenpeace;

- Council for the Protection of Rural England;
- The Royal Society for Nature Conservation;
- numerous local pressure groups that can exert great influence.

Consumers

It can be argued that environmental issues, as well as social welfare issues, come to the fore during periods of economic prosperity, and then return to a lower priority during periods of economic recession. Consumers concerns therefore may be affected by:

- economic growth;
- income levels;
- interest rates;
- exchange rates;
- employment;
- credit policies;
- income distribution;
- savings and debt;
- taxation.

As environmental issues such as climate change and sustainable development are getting more coverage in the media, there is an acceptance that being more responsible for the Earth's limited resources is a priority for the sake of future generations, even if it comes at a price. As consumer awareness grows of the environmental damage that can be caused by industry, they are being drawn, mostly by an ethical view, to purchase those products and services that are environmentally friendly or those that have EMS accreditation such as ISO 14001 (Hui et al, 2001). Banks, financial institutions and various other company stakeholders are becoming more environmentally aware about where they invest their money.

Competitors and gaining competitive advantage

The implementation of an EMS is accepted as an image-builder and business strategy to strengthen the company's competitive position. Although implementing an EMS is voluntary, using it as a means to please customers is increasingly more common (Hui et al, 2001). As competition for products and services grows, so competitors strive to be upper most in consumers' minds. The identification of shopping patterns and consumer behaviour is an important tool for winning customers. The use of sophisticated software to monitor consumers' buying habits is an attempt to maintain or create an advantage over the competitor. Identifying and anticipating changing lifestyles, such as the move towards organic food by environmentally conscious consumers, adds value to producer's products and services if they are in tune with attitudes affected by:

- the changing age structure of population;
- trends in family size;
- changes in amount and nature of leisure time;
- changes in attitude towards health and lifestyles;
- improved education;
- changes in attitudes towards family roles;
- changing work patterns;
- equal opportunities;
- culture.

It is sometimes a great temptation for companies considering the immediate benefits of having a positive environmental image to cut short the process by merely changing labels on their products and calling them environmentally friendly. Such a practice can cause greater expenditure than a change to the product or the manufacturing processes as a result of loss of business credibility and market share.

Other factors for external audits

The internet, mobile phones and e-commerce are some examples of how a company may improve its business through better communications. New developments in technology, such as automation, may lead to greater energy efficiency and waste reduction. New environmental legislation may result in harmful products such as CFCs being banned from the production process. These are just some of the operational policy changes that need to be monitored and assessed for environmental impact. Some of these factors will have a positive impact upon the environment and some will have a negative impact. A reduction in car usage to and from work will have a positive environmental impact and save people money particularly with current high fuel prices.

It is not possible to list each and every external environmental element that may result in potential opportunities or threats in the environmental audit. It is important to attempt to determine the key environmental forces and factors that need to be assessed and realize that these may vary between departments.

Sometimes the most relevant external environmental forces are not immediately obvious because new forces may develop or emerge and existing factors can change very rapidly. It is therefore prudent to keep a broad perspective on what might constitute significant environmental forces and factors and review environmental plans on a regular basis. It is important to try to forecast both the magnitude and direction of trends and changes in those external environmental factors that have been identified as most significant. It is helpful to use as many sources of information as possible to forecast possible changes, including secondary data such as that found in government or industry association statistics and trade directories.

The time scale that such forecasts encompass is important and will vary greatly depending on the sensitivity of the industry. As a rule of thumb, the time horizon for external environmental forecasting should be approximately twice as long as the duration of the corporate environmental plan that emerges from implementing the EMS.

The essence of effective environmental management involves achieving a strategic fit between the organizational activities and the threats that exist in the environment. The combination of an internal and external audit should identify key factors, consumer trends and potential changes in these factors, as well as the performance and resources of the organization. The mechanism for moving from the information gathered in the environmental management audit to using this information to develop an environmental management plan is provided by the aspects and impacts analysis discussed next. Essentially, such an analysis is used to develop a plan that builds on identified strengths and avoids or reduces environmental risk.

ASPECTS AND IMPACTS ANALYSIS

An important stage in improving the company's environmental management performance is the preparation of the aspects and impacts analysis arising from an assessment of the company's activities and processes. The identification of the environmental impacts arising from the environmental aspects will form the foundation of the targets and objectives for the corporate environmental plan.

The completed aspects and impacts analysis sheet will provide a record of the environmental effects of operating procedures, incidents, accidents and potential emergency situations that may arise. This will assist in the monitoring of their effects on the environment and the development of any necessary remedial actions and procedures. The aspects and impacts analysis provides a positive and negative record of all business activities that are environmentally significant.

The formulation of the aspects and impacts analysis sheet is completed at an early stage of implementation, but should be updated as and when required. Any new equipment brought into the company, or any process change, requires assessment for the degree of environmental impact and testing of its significance to see whether it should also be included in the analysis.

For the sake of consistency and standardization the definitions offered here are those laid down in the ISO 14000 standard. These describe an environmental aspect as 'an element of an organization's activities, products or services that can have a beneficial or adverse impact on the environment', while an environmental impact is 'the change that takes place in the environment as a result of the aspect' (CEN, 1997).

Table 2.1 *Aspects and impacts*

Item	Environmental Aspects (activity of process)	Environmental Impact	Caused By	Effect

The following list details the stages involved in aspects and impacts analysis and is discussed in detail in the following section:

- Identify and list those areas of company operations that may harm the environment.
- Classify the aspects into levels of environmental impact i.e. low, medium or high. Using a scale of 1–5 determine each impact's probability of occurrence.
- Create an aspects and impacts analysis matrix and calculate the impact scores for each aspect.
- Using a mid-score, or a cut-off score, select all those aspects above the mid-score to create the register of aspects and impacts.

Register of aspects and impacts

The register of aspects and impacts, as shown in Table 2.1, is a list that details any impacts under the following headings:

- *Item*: A serial number that is used for recording and sorting purposes.
- *Environmental aspect*: Brief details of the company's activity, product or service that can have an impact on the environment.
- *Environmental impact*: Brief description of the interaction or change.
- *Caused by*: Details of the operation, activity or process that caused the environmental interaction or change.
- *Effect*: Details of whether the environmental interaction or change has an adverse or beneficial environmental effect.

Aspects and impacts examples and description

Once the operational activities of the company have been established, all the activities and processes are listed and the list is divided into three key areas. First, activities and processes that affect the environment during normal operating procedures. Second, activities and processes that affect the environment during abnormal procedures. Third, activities and processes that affect incidents, accidents and other emergencies. This should be done in each of the three areas for:

- normal operations;
- daily operational activities or processes that are currently being carried out;
- abnormal operations;
- periodic routines that may occur in addition to the daily process and activities (these may include preventative maintenance, plant upgrades, shutdowns or silent periods);
- emergencies.

Having prepared a list the company's activities and processes (aspects) and identified their environmental impacts (both positive and negative), it is useful to introduce a measure to determine their significance, identifying and prioritizing those aspects that have a significant impact upon the environment.

Aspect and impact classification rating

For ease of explanation a five-point rating scale is used to classify each aspect's environmental impact as major, high, moderate, limited or minimal. The

Table 2.2   *Aspect classifications*

Rating	Aspect Classification	Aspect Criteria
1	Minimal	No emissions and no use of resources
		No hazardous material usage
2	Low	Low emissions and low usage of resources
		Occasional use of hazardous materials
3	Moderate	Moderate emissions and use of resources
		Moderate use of hazardous materials
4	High	High emissions and high use of resources
		High use of hazardous material
5	Major	Major emissions and major use of resources
		Major use of hazardous material

Table 2.3   *Impact classifications*

Rating	Impact Classification	Impact Criteria
1	Minimal	No noticeable environmental effect
		Effective control system already in place
		Well within discharge consent levels
2	Low	Low environmental effect
		Control system in place but could be more effective
		Well within discharge consent levels
3	Moderate	Moderate environmental effect
		Control system in place but must be improvement
		Occasionally just outside discharge consent levels
4	High	High environmental effect
		No control system in place
		Outside discharge consent levels

measurement criteria for each impact classification are shown Tables 2.2 and 2.3. A simple formula for an aspect's impact rating would be:

Overall Impact Rating = Aspect Classification Rating x Impact Classification Rating

Calculating the levels for the scales of major, high, moderate, limited or minimal will be an assessment based on existing environment agency pollution acceptance levels, experience and company size. In determining the level of resources used, the types of materials being used should be taken into consideration. The use of solder paste, particularly lead-based solder paste used to secure components in printed circuit board (PCB) assembly, for example, would typically carry a high aspect weighting. It should also be remembered that emissions can be to land, air and water.

Aspects and impacts analysis matrix

To complete the toolbox, each activity or process is assigned some degree of probability to the likelihood of the aspects and impacts occurring. Classification of an aspect can be made in the way illustrated in Table 2.4. The probability of occurrence can be measured from a score of 1 (a less than 20 per cent probability) to a score of 5 (an 80–100 per cent probability of occurrence). The calculated probability of occurrence scores are then transferred to the potential aspects and impacts probability matrix, shown in Table 2.5.

Table 2.4   *Probability of occurrence*

Score	Probability of Occurrence
5	80–100% probability
4	60–80% probability
3	40–60% probability
2	20–40% probability
1	0–20% probability

Table 2.5   *Potential aspects and impacts probability matrix*

Aspect	Probability of Occurrence	Very Good Score ← IMPACT → Bad Score											Total
		5	4	3	2	1	0	−1	−2	−3	−4	−5	
Chemical Spillage	5											X	−25
Exhaust Fumes	5								X				−10
Product Packaging	5		X										20

To determine whether the aspect has significant environmental impact multiply the probability and impact scores together. If the aspect score is less than 9, the aspect can be considered not to be significant. If the score is 9 or greater, the aspect can be considered significant. It should be noted that each process or activity may have a number of associated aspects and impacts.

Understanding the analysis matrix

The aspects that have been identified in the survey are listed on the left hand side of the matrix shown in Table 2.5. In the next column a number between 1 and 5 is put to represent the percentage of probability of the aspect occurring. The next set of columns ranging from 5 to − 5 represents the scoring system for the aspect having a positive or negative impact upon the environment. One example given in the matrix demonstrates a negative impact from a chemical spillage. A company that uses any chemicals in its operating process is likely to view any spillage as being serious; therefore a –5 score would be applied to this aspect of operations.

In contrast the reuse of packaging materials received from incoming goods can be viewed as a positive environmental impact as the same packaging materials can be used for packaging outgoing products. This would realize a score of 5 to signal a positive environmental impact.

By multiplying the scores together the figure in the furthest right column determines each aspect's impact upon the environment. The larger the negative figure, the larger the environmental impact. The larger the positive figure, the less of an impact upon the environment.

An aspect can have both positive and negative impacts upon the environment. Using the packaging example, if a significant amount of paper packaging from incoming goods was not reused, the recycling of this packaging waste would be a positive aspect but the money spent to have the packaging recycled may be a negative aspect.

Departmental analysis matrix

If larger businesses are not analysed at the level of separate departments it is virtually impossible to develop meaningful business definitions or meaningful and effective environmental management plans. It is extremely important to stress that separate parts of the environmental management plan must be developed for every department in the organization. In other words, the development of subsequent parts of the environmental management plan must be undertaken at the departmental level.

The departmental analysis enables each part of the business to have its own business definition and an example is shown in Table 2.6. For every department a business definition should specify the following elements:

- the environmental objectives for each department;
- the resources available to meet the stated objectives;
- the technology to be utilized in product or process changes.

Using a chart is a good way of visualizing the implications and magnitude of the opportunities and threats. Specific values on the bottom of the chart correspond with the total scores for each factor on the potential impact probability matrix and indicate the potential implications of each factor on the company or department.

Having created the register of aspects and impacts attention can now turn to the creation of the environmental legislation register.

REGISTER OF LEGISLATION

One result of the external audit can be a list of current legislation that has an actual or potential impact on business activities. When this list is being compiled,

Table 2.6   *Departmental aspects and impacts analysis matrix*

Give rating from 1 (lowest or poor) to 10 (highest or excellent)							
Key Environmental Factors	Weighting Factor	The Business		Department A		Department B	
		Rating	Adjusted rating	Rating	Adjusted rating	Rating	Adjusted rating
Waste generation	50	8	400	3	150	7	350
Energy usage							
Air emissions							
Total							

all legislation that can affect the company, and not just environmental laws, should be taken into consideration.

Having assessed the company's operational activities and their environmental implications, it is now possible to formulate an EMS. This begins with the creation of the list of objectives and targets, and the development of the set of management and operational procedures to ensure that the objectives and targets are achieved. The company structure is also assessed to identify those individuals within it that may be key people and to which the success of the system can be entrusted.

It is essential to be fully familiar and compliant with the regulations that apply to the company. A fundamental part of the planning and implementation process is the creation and ongoing maintenance of a register of legislation and regulations, which for ease of reference should be kept in an environmental documentation folder (EDF) for ease of reference. The register lists the regulations under the following headings:

- *Item*: A specified serial number is used for recording and sorting purposes.
- *Regulation*: Title and brief details of the regulation.
- *Issued by*: Details of the authority that has issued the regulation.
- *Dated*: The regulation issue date.
- *Applicability*: Details of the operations, activities or processes that are subject to the regulation.

In compiling and maintaining the register, the skill to be mastered is to determine which pieces of legislation affect the company's operations. In the UK there are two key acts that will apply to all companies: the Environmental Protection Act, 1990 and the Environmental Act, 1995. These two acts should be in every company's register.

Table 2.7   *Examples of objectives and targets format*

Item	Objective	Target	Method	Status
01	Completion of draft EMS documentation	Completion of draft EMS documentation, including manual, procedures, logs and forms	Follow requirements of ISO 14001 and any available examples	Complete
02	Completion of final standard EMS documentation	Issue of final standard EMS documentation	Documentation to be finalized, reviewed, approved and issued following review of drafts	Ongoing
03	Accreditation assessment preparation	Successful completion of stage assessment	Follow requirements of ISO 14001	Ongoing
04	Premises clean-up to include vehicles, tyres, containers, scrap items and oil contamination of soil and building	Removal of all potential contaminants and inherited contamination	Liaison with local council, clean-up agencies, scrap dealers and vehicle owners	Ongoing
05	Tracking and recording waste disposal, starting with recyclable paper and cardboard	Recycling and reusing as much paper and cardboard as possible	Identification of suitable haulier and use of waste collection log	Ongoing
06	Reduction in office and workshop paper and cardboard waste paper output	Noticeable reduction in waste paper and cardboard output	Publicity and placement of marked boxes throughout company, with personnel encouraged to reuse where possible and/or to avoid purchase	Ongoing
07	Reduction in office and workshop plastic waste output	Noticeable reduction in waste plastic output	Publicity and placement of marked boxes throughout company, with personnel encouraged to reuse where possible	Ongoing

Table 2.7   *Examples of objectives and targets format* (cont'd)

Item	Objective	Target	Method	Status
08	Reduction in workshop wood and metal waste output	Reuse of material and minimizing of waste output	Publicity and placement of marked boxes in company workshop, with personnel encouraged to reuse where possible	Ongoing
09	Reduction in energy consumption	Reduce energy consumption by a minimum of 10%, to include electricity and heating fuel	Personnel encouraged to make savings where possible. Improve building insulation, replace heaters and ceilings	Ongoing
10	Reduction of hazardous materials and substances	Noticeable reduction in use of hazardous materials and substances	Personnel encouraged to identify and use environmentally friendly alternatives	Ongoing
11	Reduced possibility of the emission of contaminated air	A cleaner atmosphere	Replacement of inefficient heating systems	Ongoing

OBJECTIVES AND TARGETS

The next stage of the process is to use the priorities identified in the aspects and impacts analysis to set some objectives and targets. The achievement, or the attempt to achieve, environmental objectives is the main way a company can improve its environmental performance. The objectives set do not need to be quantifiable but they do need to be realistic, identifiable and achievable. The targets are quantifiable but it may not always be easy to calculate a target. The first set of objectives and targets should reflect the introduction of the new system. As these short-term objectives are achieved so new objectives will be set, thereby creating a dynamic set that take the company through the process of continual improvement. Therefore it is necessary to be conservative in estimating savings for the first set of targets. Until the EMS has been operating for a full year it will be difficult to determine exactly how much energy has been saved or how much material has been reused. An initial annual percentage saving on the targets of 5–10 per cent is recommended. Examples of objectives and targets are given in Table 2.7.

The objectives of the EMS should encourage all employees to operate as an environmentally aware company and to demonstrate this by the employment of an effective environmental management system.

Corporate environmental plan targets list

The primary objective is to operate and maintain the company in a manner consistent with the best environmental practices, taking account of responsibilities to customers, staff, suppliers and the community at large. The objectives and targets are directly incorporated into the corporate environmental plan derived from this work. The plan should therefore be open-ended so that new objectives can be added or existing objectives changed within the programme. In the early stages this would be expected to occur on a fairly regular basis.

The list of targets that is built into the corporate environmental plan is designed to be as simple as possible, while showing complete details of goals, methods and responsibilities. The active corporate environmental plan target details should be contained in the environmental documentation folder for ease of reference.

The corporate environmental plan target details are contained in the targets list under the following headings:

- *Item*: A unique item number is assigned to each objective; this acts as a reference in reports or reviews.
- *Objective*: The specific objective is described and detailed. Some objectives may require more information, if so, this will be provided separately and a copy placed in the relevant objective's folder.
- *Target*: For example, reduce energy consumption by 10 per cent.
- *Goal*: In this context, a goal is the projected target date for completion of the objective. There needs to be flexibility built into these dates, consequently, the dates may be altered following a progress review, as may the objectives and targets.
- *Achieved*: This is the actual objective achievement date.
- *Responsibilities*: Each objective will have a person or persons designated as being responsible.
- *Comments*: This area is reserved for any pertinent comments.

ORGANIZATION AND RESPONSIBILITY

Having identified what the company wants to achieve in terms of targets and objectives, the level of employee involvement should be specified, including individuals, specific tasks and responsibilities. The type and level of resources available should also be verified to assess how achievable the objectives and targets are. Details of the training and communication programmes designed to ensure staff awareness and education should also be recorded.

Environmental Operating Procedures and Environmental Management Procedures

Operational and managerial procedures are two types of environmental management procedures. The establishment of environmental procedures is the main way in which environmental objectives and targets can be delivered. They are the basis on which the company can be sure that the requirements of the ISO 14001 standard are being adhered to because they specify the way that any and every particular activity should be undertaken. All of the procedures in the corporate environmental plan are written to guard the effective operation of the management system. Of the two sets of procedures, the operational procedures put processes into action that eventually allow the objectives and targets to be realized. The management procedures provide the controls. They ensure that the EMS is monitored continually and, where necessary, corrected and improved over time. If part of the EMS fails, the management procedures give guidance for reporting and correcting the failure.

Examples of environmental management procedures are given below and conform to ISO 14001 requirements, offering possible bases for procedure formation. The five major environmental management procedures are:

1   control of nonconformities;
2   management review;
3   corrective action;
4   document and data control;
5   internal audit.

As specified in other procedural guidelines, the start of any procedural prescription should specify the purpose of the procedure, its scope, the person responsible for its execution and its administrative process.

Examples of management procedures

Control of nonconformities
Purpose
This procedure describes how nonconformities are controlled and reported. The procedure is outlined in Figure 2.2.

Scope
This procedure establishes the way in which nonconformities are classified, recorded and evaluated.

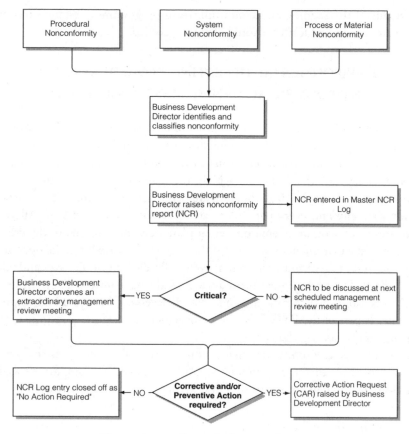

Figure 2.2   *Control of nonconformities*

Responsibility
The environmental manager is responsible for documenting nonconformities, presenting them at management review and ensuring that follow-up actions are undertaken.

Procedure
There are three types of nonconformity:

1   Procedural nonconformity – where personnel have failed to follow environmental operating procedures or other forms of instruction contained within the EMS (typically identified during internal audit or periodic review by the certifying agency), or if the nonconformity is an accident or a hazardous occurrence. The most obvious example is where someone has failed to complete a new product introduction (NPI) form when introducing a new product into the company.

2   System nonconformity – where a fault or inadequacy is identified in the EMS and change is required to assure the safety and protection of the internal and external environment. Using the NPI example again, the procedure for introducing new products into the company may not have been created.

3   Process or material nonconformity – an accident or occurrence not related to either of the above types of nonconformity (typically involving an unforeseen breakdown or failure of equipment, process or facilities). An example of this type of nonconformity may occur when a piece of machinery fails and an oil or diesel spillage creates a potentially hazardous situation from the threat of fire or water and/or land contamination.

Identification

Nonconformities may be identified by any company employee, or by anyone such as a subcontractor who may be working for the company.

Reporting

The nonconformity reporting chain is achieved through the use of existing management structures and the established interface. It may not be feasible or practical for initial reporting of a nonconformity to be done in writing. In many cases a verbal report will be made to the environmental manager who will carry out an initial investigation and then produce a written report. Unless it is impossible, all reports should be put in writing eventually, regardless of the initial method of transmission. All final nonconformity reports submitted to the environmental manager should conform to the reporting form layout distributed by the environmental manager and include details of immediate actions taken, or to be taken.

A nonconformity can be either critical or non-critical. A critical nonconformity has a direct and immediate effect on safety or protection of the environment. For example, a faulty piece of equipment might be identified or an environmental operating procedure or other form of instruction might be found to contain an error that could affect the environment. Any other type of nonconformity is, by definition, non-critical and the environmental manager has the task of deciding whether a nonconformity is critical or non-critical.

Environmental manager actions

When details of a nonconformity are received, the environmental manager should produce a nonconformity report (NCR) in which:

*   the type of nonconformity is identified;
*   the level of nonconformity is identified as critical or non-critical;
*   the nonconformity is described in sufficient detail to allow management to identify the appropriate corrective action.

Every NCR should have an issue date and be identifiable, for example by a four-digit number. The environmental manager should retain copies of all NCRs and maintain a master log of them. The log identifies NCRs by issue number and date and shows the date of the management review meeting at which the close-out actions and responsibilities would have been discussed. Each NCR is closed-out in the log by the allocation of a corrective action request (CAR) number or numbers, or when management review decides that no action is to be taken.

If the nonconformity is designated as critical, the environmental manager will call an extraordinary management review meeting as soon as possible. Temporary remedial action may also be taken immediately and detailed on the NCR. If the nonconformity is non-critical, the NCR will be presented at the next scheduled management review meeting.

Management review
Purpose
This procedure describes how management should review an EMS at regular intervals to ensure it continues to satisfy the environmental policy.

Scope
The procedure establishes the conduct by which a management review is undertaken.

Responsibility
The managing director is responsible for ensuring that the EMS is reviewed according to the procedure.

Procedure
The review should be conducted by means of a preplanned meeting chaired by the managing director, with the presence of the environmental manager and one (more if required) member of the environmental working group. Management review meetings should take place at least once in each six-month period. These meetings can be held annually depending on the company circumstances, but once very six months is recommended. The environmental manager should advise the managing director when to announce the precise date of the meeting. Unscheduled, extraordinary review meetings may also be held should circumstances dictate, particularly in the event of fire, floods and suchlike.

The environmental manager is responsible for:

- convening a management review meeting and drafting an agenda for approval by the managing director;
- maintaining the environmental records that provide input to the management review;

- ensuring that minutes of the review and all agreed actions are recorded for subsequent approval by the managing director;
- preparing and updating an EMS audit schedule for approval by the managing director.

The environmental manager should maintain an EMS audit schedule showing:

- the frequency and timing of audits;
- the specific areas and activities to be audited;
- the identity and qualification of auditor(s);
- the auditing and reporting criteria.

The EMS audit schedule should be regularly drafted and/or updated by the environmental manager for approval by the managing director. The redrafting should be carried out at least once in any 12-month period. Every company employee is responsible for compliance with the EMS audit schedule by participation, assigning resources and so forth as required.

The management review agenda should typically include:

- review of the minutes of the previous meeting and actions carried forward requiring close-out;
- results of EMS audit activity;
- review of the environmental manager's summary report of nonconformities since the previous meeting;
- review of organizational management procedures;
- review of administrative procedures;
- review of environmental operating procedures;
- review of personnel responsibilities and authority;
- review of documentation and record keeping;
- review of and adherence to EMS policies, procedures and instructions;
- need for additional familiarization or on-the-job training;
- results arising from analysis of any critical nonconformity such as personal injury, equipment damage or pollution incident;
- corrective action request close-out reports produced on non-critical and critical nonconformities since the previous meeting;
- corrective action taken on operational defects or procedural amendment in the EMS and further measures to improve its effectiveness;
- recommendations from employees and environmental working group meetings for measures to improve EMS effectiveness;
- the degree to which the environmental policy continues to meet the company's current objectives and statutory compliance requirements.

The environmental manager should revise the EMS audit schedule according to the actions arising from the management review and present to the managing director for approval. The results of the review should be brought to the attention of those persons responsible for implementing the proposed changes.

All actions arising from a management review should be closed-out and signed off by the managing director.

Continuous improvement

Monitoring and measuring the existing environmental management plan is a necessary requirement of ISO 14001. A similar requirement of the standard is a programme or system that facilitates continual environmental improvement. It is too simplistic to set a number of targets and objectives, achieve them, then sit back. Once existing targets and objectives have been achieved, more need to be set. These future targets and objectives may take the form of new targets based on existing objectives, for example a further 5 per cent saving on energy usage, or completely new objectives and targets.

As mentioned at the outset, energy savings or waste minimization levels can be too ambitious, annual goals should instead be achievable. It is better to have achieved an extra 5 per cent savings targets each year than a 25 per cent one-year target. The latter may well be difficult to achieve in one year, and yet failure to do so may have a negative effect on morale and the programme of continuous improvement.

Corrective action

Purpose

This procedure describes how corrective and preventive action is initiated and maintained within the EMS, and is outlined in Figure 2.3.

Scope

The procedure establishes the way in which corrective and preventive action is documented and reviewed.

Responsibility

The environmental manager is responsible for producing a corrective action request for any corrective action decided at a management review.

Procedure

The CAR provides brief details of the nonconformity to which the corrective action relates and provides information on what needs to be done. It identifies the addressee – the person required to complete the corrective action – and includes a time-scale for completion of the corrective action.

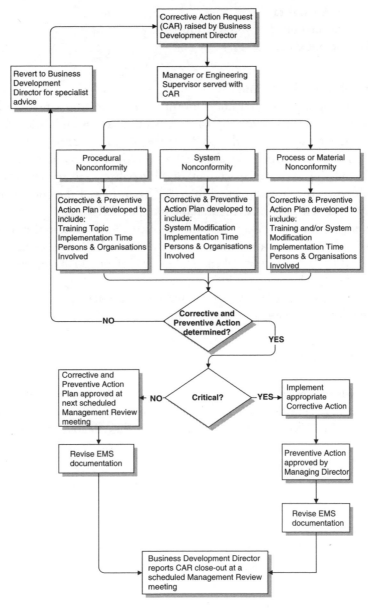

Figure 2.3   *Corrective action process*

The environmental manager should retain copies of all CARs issued and maintain a log of CARs that shows:

- CAR number;
- nonconformity report relating to the CAR;
- addressee;

- date the CAR was raised;
- CAR status (actioned or to be actioned);
- CAR close-out date.

Close-out of corrective actions

CARs relating to a procedural nonconformity are closed-out when the auditor, who raised the NCR, has reviewed the corrective action and accepted that it addresses the requirements of the NCR. If the original auditor is not available, the environmental manager may close-out a procedural nonconformity.

CARs relating to cases of system or material/process nonconformity are closed-out when the environmental manager has reviewed the corrective action and accepted that it satisfies the requirements of the NCR.

The environmental manager should produce a CAR close-out report on all closed-out CARs. This report briefly summarizes the NCR, the corrective action required and the actual action taken. The environmental manager should retain copies of all CAR close-out reports.

Copies of CAR close-out reports should be distributed to management at the next scheduled management review meeting.

Document and data control

Purpose

This procedure, shown in Figure 2.4, describes the control of documents and means of electronic data control (including indexing, data storage and protection, and archiving) that are essential to the effective operation of the EMS.

Scope

The procedure should apply to the following:

- environmental management procedures;
- environmental operating procedures;
- forms and reports;
- work or other instructions;
- any other environmental documentation.

Responsibility

The issue, amendment, approval and distribution of all EMS documentation should be carried out under the direction and authority of the environmental manager. Document holders are responsible for the maintenance of controlled documentation and for ensuring that all obsolete documentation is returned as instructed.

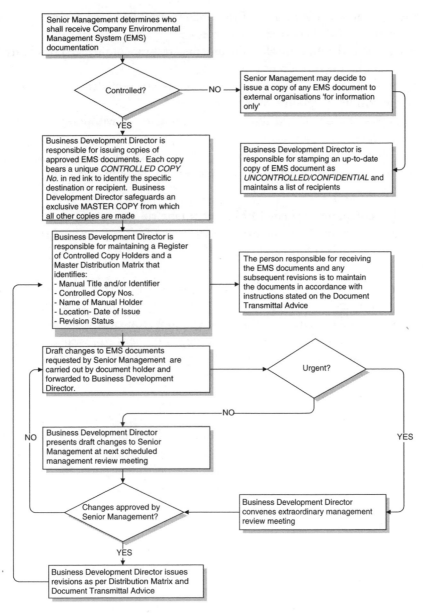

Figure 2.4   *Document and data control*

Procedure

All documents relevant to the EMS should be reviewed, maintained and controlled. It is necessary that:

• documents and their subsequent revisions are reviewed and approved by the environmental manager prior to use;

- the issue and revision status of the documented EMS is known to all users through the use of controlled documents;
- persons issued with controlled documents are aware of their responsibility for maintaining the revision records;
- up-to-date issues of appropriate documents are provided at any locations where critical operations are performed;
- all copies of obsolete and superseded documents are withdrawn from use to be destroyed or archived;
- any obsolete documents retained as records are identified suitably and that a master list is maintained of all documents and data under control.

Control of company originated EMS documentation

All documents should bear a control header design for the procedure that should include (in designated form and location):

- a corporate identifier (as appropriate), document title, chapter number and title;
- issue status such as draft or the date (expressed as month and year);
- revision number, starting at 00 and increasing sequentially in units;
- page number, or chapter number and page number (expressed as x or x-xx), or page number and total number of pages per chapter (expressed as x/xx);
- a unique numbering sequence to indicate the function of forms.

Distribution matrix

The environmental manager should maintain a distribution matrix that records the information in the list about all documentation relevant to the EMS. Any changes affecting the location and/or status of individual publications or copies should also be recorded on the distribution matrix:

- document title;
- controlled copy number;
- location/holder;
- revision status;
- issue date.

Document transmittal advice

When a publication or document is issued, or if a revision is issued by the environmental manager, it should be accompanied by a document transmittal advice form. This form is addressed to the person who is to receive the new publication or who is responsible for revising an existing publication.

If the form accompanies a new publication, the recipient is required to signify receipt and respond in accordance with the instruction given on the form. The revision record is to be completed and signed in accordance with the document transmittal advice form instructions, which also detail the response required.

Revision record
Other than forms and minor documents, company originated EMS publications are prefaced by a revision record. This is a record of revisions to the specific publication and, therefore, provides essential evidence that a publication is being maintained up to date. It is the responsibility of the person having charge of the publication to ensure that the record is maintained correctly and accurately.

Control of electronic data
All electronic data that originates from within the company must be identified, indexed and stored in accordance with current company instructions. Access to company computer systems should be granted only to authorized persons. Access to computer files should be similarly controlled. Such precautions can minimize the possibility of accidental or deliberate corruption of essential information, or electronic infestation that might corrupt or destroy data.

Control of documents from external sources
The environmental manager should be required to maintain an up-to-date list of all externally supplied publications and should also be responsible for the purchase and supply of such publications.

Each publication should be given a unique number or code upon receipt. The date of issue should be clearly stated. Obsolete copies should be withdrawn from service and marked 'superseded' prominently on the front cover.

Internal audit
Purpose
This procedure describes how internal audits of the EMS are scheduled, planned, carried out and recorded.

Scope
The procedure establishes the conduct by which internal audits are undertaken.

Responsibility
The EMS is subject to regular audit to ensure that it continues to meet its objectives and that personnel are complying with procedures and work instructions. The environmental manager is responsible for scheduling and documenting audits. All company personnel are responsible for assisting the audit process by participating and assigning resources as required.

Procedure

The environmental manager should draw up an audit schedule that defines the number, frequency and subjects of audits of the EMS. This schedule takes account of work scheduling and any other critical activities, and includes, as a minimum, at least one audit of the EMS every year. The environmental manager should nominate a suitably qualified person to act as auditor and should make known to all employees the name and location of the auditor on company notice boards.

The completed audit schedule will need to be approved at a management review before it can be put into action.

Prior to the audit, the auditor should decide what particular aspects of the EMS are to be audited and what objective evidence is to be sought. All persons and/or departments to be audited need to be notified at least one week in advance of the planned date of the audit. The subject of the audit, that is, the particular procedure(s) or work instruction(s) to be covered, and any personnel to whom the auditor needs to talk, should be clearly identified.

During the audit, the auditor examines objective evidence to confirm that operations are being carried out as required by procedures and work instructions. The auditor also discusses procedures and work instructions with personnel and evaluates any corrective action taken relating to CARs, with a view to authorizing close-out. Following the audit, the auditor produces an audit report, which should include:

- date, time and location of the audit;
- objective of the audit;
- basis of the audit (those procedures and work instructions that were verified);
- details of personnel audited;
- details (including NCR numbers) of any nonconformity noted;
- details (including CAR numbers) of any corrective action evaluated.

If nonconformities are found, a follow-up audit may be conducted to ensure that corrective action has been successful. Alternatively, the corrective action may be reviewed at the next scheduled audit. The environmental manager is responsible for deciding whether a follow-up audit is required, but one will be required and conducted for all critical nonconformities.

Copies of the audit report should be provided to the auditee(s) and to all members of senior management involved in management review. The environmental manager retains copies of reports and completed audits should be discussed at the next scheduled management review meeting.

MONITORING AND MEASURING

An important part of establishing and maintaining the effectiveness of the corporate environmental plan is ensuring that the company's significant environmental impacts are being controlled on a daily basis. The process of monitoring and measuring generates information to ensure that control and continuous improvement occurs. Monitoring and measuring should occur at regular intervals within the stages of implementing the EMS. Once the objectives and targets are set, responsibility has been allocated and the operational and managerial procedures are in place, the opportunity arises to monitor and measure the EMS in preparation for the EMS audit to evaluate its effectiveness.

The following sections describe some of the documentation and review processes used to monitor and measure the progression of the EMS, including:

- annual environmental management reports;
- environmental plan reviews and control processes;
- identification of environmental performance indicators;
- opportunity and threat analysis;
- evaluation of previous corporate environmental plans.

Environmental management reports

Presenting an annual environmental management report provides an opportunity to review how successfully targets and objectives are being achieved, and to assess the way in which the environmental management planning function is intended to operate. The environmental report has been identified as a key tool in communicating environmental performance to employees and stakeholders and therefore improving staff morale and corporate image (Ramus, 1998; 2002). The report functions as a monitoring and measuring device by providing a point of reference, or bench mark, against which to measure the progress made since setting the targets and objectives. An outline of the control and evaluation mechanisms helps to assess or evaluate current and previous environmental management plans. The issue and control of documentation is important to the effective monitoring and control of environmental procedures. Quality control documents may already exist within the current control procedures of the company and these should be used to avoid repetition and extra work.

Environmental plan review and control aims

Four of the most common aims of the plan review and control processes are:

- to permit problems or developments that do not match planned or budgeted schedule, to be identified early and addressed if required;
- to identify their causes and act to nullify their effects;
- to provide input into the ongoing environmental management function of identifying environmental management aspects and impacts;
- to act as a performance indicator and stimulus for environmental management personnel.

Control mechanisms may include or involve the development of:

- performance criteria and standards;
- acceptable ranges within which these criteria and standards can be deemed to have been satisfied;
- procedures to provide suitable and reliable measures of results;
- the means to compare the results achieved with the standards and criteria set;
- systems that enable effective corrective measures to be taken;
- a reliable means of forecasting outcomes.

The degree to which budgeted targets for each product within the corporate portfolio are realized, measured by value and volume, should usually be checked month by month. A system (an existing budgetary system would suffice) must be established to enable the production of reliable and useful data as a matter of routine and as and when it is needed.

Data must be available at the appropriate level, for example aggregated figures showing the savings derived through implementation of the EMS, and detailed by department if required. Budget responsibilities need to be clearly delineated; for example a clear budget responsibility should be specified for the environmental management function to encourage accountability.

Plan review meetings can also function as occasions on which certain kinds of information can be disseminated. For example environmental management research data, which may have been commissioned on behalf of one department, may not easily 'trickle across' in less formal situations.

Controls should also operate over new product development, with specific reviews of the development of such products or services. Continued shortfalls against projected performance should trigger revision or remedial activity.

Environmental performance indicators

As the aspects and impacts of an organization vary according to its business activities, so the creation of environmental performance indicators (EPI) must vary. The following sections list possible EPIs that should be measured.

Resource usage measure

This measure provides an insight into the consumption of energy, water and other resources at the organizational, departmental and process levels. Examples include:

- tonnage of raw materials used per unit of production;
- percentage of recycled or reused materials per unit of production;
- energy consumption per unit of production.

Emissions/waste measure

There are no generally accepted guidelines for measuring or reporting emission levels. However, once operating under the ISO 14001, EMS organizations are required to demonstrate continual improvement. Monthly spreadsheets and graphs provide suitable evidence to demonstrate emissions of effluent per unit of production and the percentage of paper or cardboard recycled or reused per unit of production.

Environmental impact measure

This measure assesses the impact the organization's activities have upon the environment. For example transport companies may measure the emissions of carbon dioxide from vehicles (emission/waste measure) but may not measure the degree of impact carbon dioxide has on ozone depletion.

Environmental risk measure

The increasing amount of environmental legislation and regulation is a key driver for most organizations seeking to reduce the probabilities of an environmental accident, such as a tanker oil spill. It is too simplistic for an organization to arbitrarily state that there is a 15 per cent chance of a major incident in the next three years without undertaking an environmental risk assessment exercise.

Management systems measure

The degree of management input into a new environmental system can be a useful measure of innovation. The introduction of new manufacturing procedures may create significant cost savings from improved processes or create new products or service opportunities.

Customer measure

Customer measurement should pervade all organizations. The company must:

- identify its target customers;
- convey the needs of these customers;
- show how its products and services satisfy these needs.

Competitor measure

It is also useful to conduct a competitor analysis to help understand relative strengths and weaknesses. This involves the identification and weighting of operating factors to determine their relative importance in the industry. When all weights are added together the total should reach 100. Each success factor must then be assessed against other major competitors on a scale from one (a low or poor competitiveness rating) to ten (a high or excellent competitive rating).

Adjusted competitiveness ratings are calculated by multiplying the weighting factor by the individual company's ratings. Total company competitiveness ratings are calculated by adding together the adjusted ratings for each success factor for each company. To determine competitor ratings use Table 2.6 (departmental aspects and impact analysis matrix) above and change the departmental classification to competitors.

Efficiency measure

There can be many levels of corporate activity where efficiency measures could be applied. Taking a holistic view of the organization, the ratio of total inputs (such as energy and resources) to total outputs (such as products and services) can be calculated. At operational level, the measurement of energy efficiency is also important. It is a simple process to calculate the bottom line energy cost with the following formula:

$$\frac{\text{total cost of energy bill}}{\text{number of kWh used}} = \text{cost per kWh}$$

Another method of measuring efficiency is the plant load factor (PLF) and is represented by the following formula:

$$\frac{\text{annual consumption of kWh x 100}}{\text{maximum demand (kW) x hours in the year}} = \text{PLF}$$

Improving the PLF will reduce the supply price and therefore reduce manufacturing costs.

Financial measure

This measure can be as simple as recording the costs associated with dealing with an environmental issue or implementing an EMS. It may be introduced at the time of setting environmental budgets and, together with a method of exception reporting, as and when there are significant over- or underspends.

Impacts measure

Direct measures of emissions or waste indicate the impact of operational activities upon the environment. For example, samples of discharged water can be collected and independently analysed. The quantity of emissions found provide benchmark levels of contaminants that can either be reduced or completely eliminated.

Opportunity and threat analysis

A good way of thinking about the implications and magnitude of impacts is to reflect upon them as opportunities or threats by using Figure 2.5. Specific values on the bottom of the chart correspond with the total scores for each factor on the

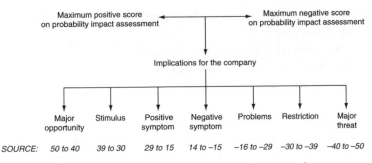

Figure 2.5 *Impact opportunity or threat analysis*

potential aspects and impacts probability matrix (Table 2.6) and indicate the potential implications of each factor on the company or department.

The evaluation process of previous management plans

In order to regulate and control the environmental management plan effectively, environmental reports or other company information can be used to locate the causes of underperformance precisely, and to spot those aspects that are working and that the environmental management plan is therefore getting right.

Two main types of measure can be employed: environmental management costs to sales ratios and customer tracking.

Environmental management costs to sales ratios

This ratio relates the amount spent on environmental management activities to the sales that have been achieved by the company. This is an important, but broad, measure that must be interpreted carefully; it provides a detailed check on environmental management expenditure. An example could be to state that acceptable annual environmental management costs should equate to 2 per cent of sales revenues.

Customer tracking

As with marketing and advertising initiatives, it is important to monitor how customers feel about the company's products and its environmental management activities. Such tracking includes a wide range of qualitative and quantitative measures of customer reactions taken from panel data, internal records of customer complaints, sales force reports, focus group interviews and surveys.

Because each business is different, it is difficult to outline a standard system for evaluating performance. The following list may help:

- What has happened since the previous environmental management plan?
- How does this accord with the timescale or programme indicated in the previous environmental management plan?

- How does it measure up to intended progress?
- Why has this happened?
- What extra costs (if any) have been incurred?
- How does it fit into the budgeted figures?
- What actions are required as a result?

Of course this may be the first environmental management plan and there may be little or nothing to compare it to. If a previous environmental plan exists, a simple review would assess whether previously specified targets and objectives have been achieved. If they have, some new ones should be set, if they have not, it is necessary to find out why not. The ethos of continuous improvement on which the ISO 14001 standard is based must be evident within environmental plans. That said, targets and objectives should not be a huge burden that is impossible for the company to achieve.

The production of corporate environmental annual reports means little if the organization does not have the ability to measure its performance. Having prepared a list of activities and processes (aspects) and identified their environmental impacts (both positive and negative), it is useful to introduce a measure to determine their significance and to set benchmarks to determine whether progress is being made.

The implementation of an environmental management system is of no benefit to an organization unless it can demonstrate to external, independent observers and stakeholders that improvements are being made. The collection of detailed data from clear EPI, over time, provides a vehicle with which an organization can set benchmarks and demonstrate through catalogued evidence that continuous environmental improvement is being made.

ENVIRONMENTAL MANAGEMENT SYSTEM AUDIT

The environmental audit that occurs at the early stages of implementing an EMS is concerned with assessing the external and internal environmental issues of the company. The EMS audit assesses whether the performance of the environmental management system conforms to the planned objectives and the requirements of the ISO 14001 standard. Any recommendations for change to the system will generally follow this system audit. Findings from the audit should be discussed and actioned at the management review.

The next section explores the audit procedure for testing the EMS and for establishing a management review format to determine further development or changes to the system. Figure 2.6 demonstrates the number of elements involved in controlling the efficient functioning of the EMS.

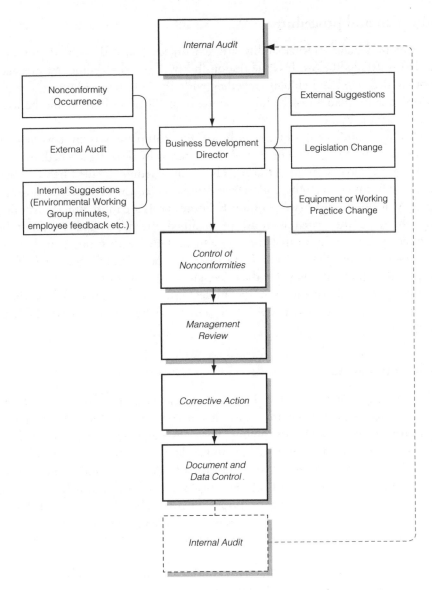

Figure 2.6   *Environmental management procedure overview*

The EMS audit will help determine whether:

- the business activities are conforming to the requirements of the EMS;
- there is employee awareness, together with procedural familiarity and compliance;
- there is operational relevance, accuracy and effectiveness of the EOP and EMP;
- there is proper determination of the EMS adequacy by senior management.

Audit plan and procedure

The way in which internal audits are scheduled, planned, carried out and recorded is detailed below. It is the responsibility of the environmental manager (or other dedicated individual), together with that of the working group, to develop an audit plan and schedule. A suitably qualified auditor should be used to undertake the audit.

This final audit requires an audit of the complete system covering all operations of the company. The best place to start is by devising a schedule of all the audits that have to be undertaken. The audit schedule detailed below shows that the audit functions to be undertaken can be spread throughout the year at a frequency of either one or two per month. Some audits are more time consuming than others, so the schedule must be planned carefully. Audits should be scheduled systematically so that they are all completed within one year. During the implementation phase of any EMS there will be economic trade-offs. One example of a trade-off may be the acceptance of low prioritization, or late response by some departments when implementing environmental procedures due to operational requirements. A late response may be considered preferable to no response.

Audit notification

Under the requirements of the ISO 14001 standard, regular audits of the EMS need to be carried out to ensure that it continues to meet its objectives and that personnel are complying with management and operational procedures. Prior to any audit being undertaken, each person to be audited must be notified a minimum of one week in advance of the audit date. It may also be useful to post a list of all employees to be audited, including times and dates, on the company notice boards. The notification of audits may seem like a minor piece of auditing etiquette, but the assessor will want proof of audit notifications and a nonconformity will result if they are not found.

The audit notification requirements can be very simple in format but must provide advance notification of the following:

- who will be audited;
- when and where the audit will take place;
- details of the topics to be covered by the audit.

In addition to the above requirements a brief note as to how each person is to answer the audit questions and where the answers can be located would also prove to be time well spent. It is always helpful to spell out the audit requirements clearly and in full. Audits can at times be viewed with suspicion and trepidation so time taken to reassure will aid the process and improve results. Set a completion date for all persons to be audited. This will ensure that all audits are completed quickly. Audit times may not suit everyone and some will change. Having a final completion date will help ensure that any time changes remain within the allotted time period.

Audit questions

Table 2.8 is an example of an audit questionnaire that could be applied. The presentation is simple with space available for answers. Prior notification of any audit allows each person being audited the opportunity to dash to the nearest environmental manual and familiarize themselves with the relevant procedures.

When setting the audit questions it is necessary to choose whether to make them difficult or simple. The benefit of the simple option is that people feel less threatened by the task and are more inclined to take time to read the relevant procedures. The audit can be simplified by warning the individual of the systems and procedures to be audited. Due to operational pressures most employees appreciate more direction and less reading of procedures. This does not diminish the exercise. The audit procedure is more than likely to be a new system and therefore a learning experience for everyone. With good use of time and communication everyone will come to understand what is required of them and how the new system works.

During the audit, the auditor will examine:

- the organizational structure;
- management and operational procedures;
- the work place including layout and operations;
- how well the EMS meets the requirements of the company's environmental objectives.

It is highly unlikely that an EMS will be audited without incurring one or more nonconformity. In fact, the more nonconformities found the better the system will be and the more satisfied the assessor will be. The audit process thus provides two key benefits: first, demonstrating that the EMS works and, second and more importantly, demonstrating the working of the management procedure by identifying, raising and actioning nonconformities.

Audit report

Having completed the audit, evidence is required. The construction of an audit report is the next task. This provides the assessor with two pieces of evidence of a successfully working procedure and system. The first is the proof that an audit

Table 2.8 *Example of an audit questionnaire*

Question	Answer
Who is responsible for the identification, handling and storage of all waste?	
What procedure defines the methods to be used for the handling, storage and disposal of liquid and solid waste produced in the office, workshop and stores areas of the company?	
Who is responsible for documenting and managing the environmental management system?	
Where would information be found regarding the way in which spillages of hazardous materials should be dealt with?	
Who is responsible for the storage of all materials?	
What is the name of the plan that is designed to be a dynamic and open-ended list of objectives and goals for the company to achieve, in accordance with ISO 14001?	
What is the correct method for the disposal of waste categorized as rubbish?	
Who is responsible for the storage and maintenance of all records and completed forms that are part of the EMS?	
Who is responsible for ensuring that personnel are adequately trained and are competent before carrying out any process or operation?	
What environmental documentation is required following the introduction of a new process, product or substance within the company?	

has been carried out in accordance with the auditing procedure. The second is the proof that those employees audited have read the procedures and are familiar with the general requirements of their role in the EMS.

The audit report should consist of three elements:

- a cover sheet;
- the response to the audit questions;
- the conclusions of the auditor.

In effect the audit is the company's annual medical check-up. The audit report contains details of individual environmental audits that have been conducted in accordance with the requirements of the EMS auditing procedure.

Box 2.1 Template for audit report

Auditee: Auditor:

Audit Date: Audit Location:

Audit Objective: Audit Report Number:

	Yes	No	
NCR			NCR Number:
CAR			CAR Number:
Follow-up Action Required? (see narrative)			Reference Number:

Narrative:

Signed (Auditor):   Date:

MANAGEMENT REVIEW

If the company is to achieve continual environmental improvement, the environmental plan needs to be reviewed and examined regularly. The review should not be seen to be restrictive but should encompass all aspects of the environmental management system. It should be viewed as a health check for the well-being of the system.

The senior management team should carry out an annual review of the EMS in order to ensure its continuing suitability and effectiveness. These reviews establish the need, if any, to change policy, procedures, controls, objectives or other relevant matters, taking account of the audit results, changing circumstances, including legislation and the need for continual improvement. The management review should discuss every element of the EMS to ensure that each is working effectively. Future objectives and targets will need to be identified and discussed during the review. The commitment of senior management is most in evidence at the management review. Every decision made by the senior managers present at the review is accepted by all and the managing director ratifies the minutes of the management review.

The existing policy statement also needs to be reviewed annually by the managing director who should update the contents in order to stress the commitment of the company towards continually improving environmental performance.

A major outcome of the initial environmental review should be the formation of an environmental working group (EWG) headed by a senior manager or director. The EWG should be tasked with meeting at least once a month in order to discuss any matters that have arisen and to progress any ongoing environmental topics. Meetings can be arranged more frequently if the need arises, particularly if the plan is to introduce the EMS quickly.

Employee involvement in environmental matters is fundamental to the adoption and maintenance of a successful EMS. A number of ways in which employee involvement in the EMS could be improved should be proposed, including a survey for suggestions as to how the company's operations for environmental protection could be strengthened. In addition, all employees should be urged to highlight any process or operation that could have any adverse environmental impact.

Environmental management review minutes

Box 2.2 presents an example of review meeting minutes. Minutes are crucial for providing evidence that the review has taken place, and also ensure that the issues raised are acted upon.

Box 2.2 Example of review meeting minutes

Date/time:
Location:
Present:

Item	Topic	Action
01	Initial meeting. Consequently, there were no previous minutes to review and no previous actions had been carried forward.	
02	Reported on personnel audit progress and discussed the proposed audit schedule.	
03	The two NCRs that had been submitted were discussed. CAR action had been initiated.	
04	The use and effectiveness of EMPs was discussed. No problems or difficulties arose.	
05	The use and effectiveness of EOPs were discussed. No problems or difficulties arose.	
06	Personnel responsibilities were discussed and were considered adequate. No points arose.	
07	Documentation and record keeping were discussed. Current standards were considered adequate, and no points arose.	
08	The need for additional familiarization and training was discussed. Current levels were considered adequate. No points arose.	
09	No critical nonconformities were raised to date. No points arose.	
10	The two current CARs were discussed. Recommended actions would be initiated by the environmental manager.	
11	No employee or working group recommendations or suggestions have been received.	
12	The functionality of the environmental plan was discussed and it was agreed that no changes were required at this stage	

Minutes prepared by:

Authenticated: Environmental Manager

Minutes agreed: Managing Director

Extraordinary management review meeting

Any person within the company can, and should, report an actual or potential environmental nonconformity. All nonconformities should be reported directly to a senior manager, either in person or in writing. The senior manager should discuss the report with the originator and assist in the accurate recording of the nonconformity. If a critical nonconformity is identified (that is, if it has an immediate and direct effect on safety or protection of the environment), immediate preventive action should be taken by a responsible person. Following consultation with the senior manager or director, an extraordinary management review meeting may be convened in order to approve further corrective action. Each nonconformity is evaluated at a management review meeting where it is decided if corrective action is required or any prior action taken has achieved this aim. The management review process also examines the EMS as a whole to ensure that it continues to meet the objectives of the corporate environmental policy.

Corrective action

Corrective action is the action taken by a responsible person under the direction of a senior manager to prevent the recurrence of a nonconformity or to improve the EMS. Corrective action is formalized by:

- revision to the EMS documentation;
- issuing the changed documentation;
- initiating a follow-up audit to verify implementation and effectiveness of the corrective action;
- internal audit.

The cycle of activities is completed when the corrective actions are closed-out under the internal audit procedure. The role of the senior manager in the cycle of nonconformity reporting, the implementation of corrective action, follow-up audit and document control is essential to the effective operation of the EMS.

THE CORPORATE ENVIRONMENTAL PLAN

The corporate environmental plan is the culmination of the auditing process. Having gone through the identifying, listing, analysing and prioritizing of the operational aspects and their environmental impacts, the emergent targets and objectives will form the basis of the corporate environmental plan. The corporate environmental plan should be designed to be a dynamic and open-ended list of objectives and targets. Some of the initial targets and objectives set in the early stages of introducing an environmental management system will be realized upon accreditation of ISO 14001. One of the first objectives listed may be the achievement of an environmental management standard.

In short, some objectives and targets will have completion deadlines, and when achieved these should be deleted from the corporate plan and replaced with new objectives and targets. Because the management review is done on an annual basis operational activities may change and this will necessitate the introduction of new targets and objectives. The process of reviewing and restating environmental objectives and targets offers the opportunity for continuous operational and environmental improvements to be made.

As with the previous stages of the process, the plan must be regularly reviewed and updated by the environmental manager in consultation with the EWG. The managing director will also carry out a periodic review of the EMP. Periodic progress reports should be circulated within the company.

An environmental management plan should be easy to read and avoid jargon wherever possible. Most of the people reading the plan will not be environmental management experts. If complicated terminology is used, definitions and explanatory notes should be included. In some cases a glossary of terms is necessary and should be included as a separate section at the end of the environmental management plan.

Each section and page should be numbered so that the reader can easily navigate the plan. Visual aids such as tables, charts and diagrams are often the best way to convey complex information. Photographs of the products, processes and business activities can be used to give life to the environmental management plan. When conducting forecasts and writing the environmental management plan budget, it is advisable to be candid and honest. Over-optimism can cause doubt in the reader's mind about the credibility and judgement of the author.

When the first draft of the corporate environmental plan is complete it should be checked for inconsistencies. For example the environmental management aspects and impacts and environmental management procedures should be in line with the company's objectives and targets. At this stage it is also necessary to check that the content of the environmental management plan is relevant to the reader, with any surplus material discarded. It is also vital that the objectives are communicated and wherever possible agreed with those who are charged with the responsibility of achieving them.

Typically, companies have operational objectives affecting many areas of the company, any one of which can affect the selection of environmental management objectives and strategies. The business objectives are likely to encompass more than finance and be of both a qualitative and quantitative nature. Some of the more common objectives for organizations include:

Qualitative	Quantitative
• market standing/reputation;	• profitability through materials recycling;
• innovation;	• greater production efficiency;
• management performance;	• profitability through energy efficiency;
• public responsibility;	• identification of new products;
• organizational development.	• efficient operational processes.

When framing the objectives it is necessary to make clear how they will be achieved. For example an objective to increase market share with a low product price may be written as: 'Our objective is to decrease energy consumption by 10 per cent in the following year by conducting an extensive energy usage analysis and supplier cost comparison.' Objectives should be achievable and made relevant to the purpose of the plan, making sure that they are in line with the financial projections and all other aspects of the environmental plan.

THE AUDIT OF ENVIRONMENTAL MANAGEMENT OBJECTIVES, POLICIES AND ACTIVITIES

From time to time the company should conduct a complete review of environmental management objectives, policies and activities on a company-wide basis. Such a review is perhaps the most comprehensive approach to evaluating environmental management effectiveness. The review aims to examine and evaluate the success or otherwise of the environmental management objectives and policies that have been guiding the company. It is a comprehensive review of both the activities of the company in relation to environmental management, and also the environmental factors that are likely to bear upon their success or failure in achieving the objectives of the environmental management plan.

ENVIRONMENTAL MANAGEMENT PLAN BUDGET

The environmental management plan budget is crucial as it provides the basis on which key strategic and funding decisions are based. Therefore it is important that it is accurate and well presented. When writing the financial element of the plan it is essential to describe the environmental management budget and the ways in which it relates to the targets that were developed earlier in the environmental management plan. It should include a statement of the funds required, their intended purpose and the projected impact on the profitability of the business.

Budgets and resources are allocated in an attempt to meet business and environmental management objectives and to make the overall environmental management plan successful. Products performing particularly well or particularly poorly, from an environmental perspective, will obviously require quite different levels of activity, and consequently, differential allocation of budgetary resources.

Often the costs involved in the environmental management plan are a very significant part of the overall operating costs of a company's operation. It is sensible to plan these costs systematically, to attempt to forecast their effect, and to keep as close control as is possible over the way in which they are used.

The budget section should be kept brief but comprehensive. The environmental management budget can be as comprehensive as a financial plan that would be written as part of a business plan. Many of the items may be identical and could be transferred directly from the business plan or profit and loss forecast.

Key tasks to be undertaken to develop an environmental management plan budget include estimating total revenue and costs, and allocating environmental management resources within the portfolio of products/services and between elements of the environmental management objectives.

Although there are a number of different ways to calculate an environmental management plan budget, the environmental management plan follows a staged procedure to undertake each of these tasks in turn.

Estimating total revenue and costs

A profit and loss forecast is useful to show what is left after all the money that enters the company has been spent. The profit and loss forecast has to be produced before the environmental management plan. Indeed, if an acceptable level of net profit is not achieved for any product at the end of this stage then it will be necessary to revisit assumptions made elsewhere in the plan. In this way, the actual figures will determine how the business is run. The first stage of the environmental management plan budget involves using this information to calculate total revenue and costs as well as gross and net profit.

There are three key variables to be aware of, in addition to revenue from customers:

- costs of product or process (direct costs);
- all other non-environmental management overheads;
- environmental management budget.

Direct costs
Direct costs are expenses that are directly attributable to the procurement or manufacture of the products. They include:

- hire of factory plant and equipment;
- salaries of production-related people (factory workers, production manager, etc.);
- manufacturing utility costs (gas, electricity, water);
- distribution or transportation costs.

All other non-environmental management overheads

Any expenses not directly attributable to the sale of an individual product are called overheads; these costs are not directly needed to manufacture the products sold. Some costs are extremely hard to define and may need to be split between direct costs and overhead classifications. Other examples of environmental management overheads include:

- management salaries;
- office rent and rates;
- insurance;
- leasing and rental of office equipment.

When calculating the costs of implementing and EMS, consider simultaneously the decisions that need to be made with regard to the level of available company resources, as this will directly influence the size of the environmental management budget.

Allocation of the environmental management budget

The environmental management budget has to be allocated to the various departments or elements of the environmental management plan. New products, or products that the company is attempting to reposition environmentally, may require a higher environmental management budget commitment than others. Estimates of additional revenue for new environmentally friendly products or by-products should help to make the allocation decisions a little easier.

The costs of distribution and production are accounted for under the estimates of total costs, however, there will be a need to calculate budgets for promotion, environmental management research and new product development. When these budgets are set, the theory of 'diminishing returns' is generally used. Extra spending on promotion, environmental management research or new product development should generate increases in returns in the long run at least equal to the expenditures. Further expenditure is justified only to the point when the marginal return effectively ceases to exist. It is important to outline progress payments for parts of the environmental management budget. Costs may occur on a phased basis over different timescales, for example weekly, monthly or quarterly.

As part of the environmental management budget it is useful to calculate:

- value added per employee;
- cost per employee;
- cost per product or process.

It is possible to extend this list substantially. Every business has its own unique environmental characteristics, philosophy of management, culture, objectives and methods of working, so it is easy to imagine new 'measures' or other ways of using the environmental management budget.

ISO 14001 cost guide

Calculating the costs of introducing ISO 14001 into a company, can be summarized as follows.

Direct costs

The direct costs are readily accessible and easy to calculate. These include the registration fee and the annual audit costs. The registration fee is a signing-on fee that covers the administration and paperwork issued to a company when joining an accreditation body. The fee is not refundable if progress is halted or the accreditation company is changed.

One way of speeding up the implementation process and limiting the likelihood of failure is to have an extra assessment day prior to assessment stages two and three. Pre-assessment assessments only require the presence of one assessor. The benefit of extra assessment days is that indirect costs can be saved by reducing the time required for implementation. Also motivation levels tends to stay higher and agendas are less likely to change with a shorter implementation period.

To ensure standards are maintained and continually improved, an annual audit is mandatory under ISO 14000 guidelines leading to annual audit costs. For those companies achieving the standard for the first time, audits are required biannually for the first two years.

Indirect costs

The extent of the indirect costs will depend on levels of enthusiasm and the size of the environmental budget. It will also depend on the size of the working group (the bigger the group the bigger the overhead allocation) how often group meetings are held and how long they last.

3
Organizational Barriers

INTRODUCTION

This chapter investigates organizational barriers to environmental management systems and the extent to which the barriers facilitate or impede the implementation of an EMS. The identification of key organizational barriers can assist management in allocating scarce resources. It is suggested that resources can be allocated more efficiently and effectively if those barriers that facilitate the implementation of an EMS can be distinguished from those that impede the EMS.

BACKGROUND

The identification of barriers to EMS implementation is necessary to enable corporate corrective countermeasures. However, corporate managers are finding themselves with an increasing number of barriers to counter if environmental management systems are to be introduced successfully. Tackling all of the identified obstacles may be considered an inefficient use of resources, particularly if some barriers have a greater impact than others. Managers may welcome a more analytical approach that endeavours to identify key barriers on which scarce resources can be focused to achieve the greatest benefits.

Corporations at the early stages of implementing an environmental management system could be aided by the identification and measurement of those barriers that are likely to emerge during the process. Such measurement would allow corrective action to be taken with greater precision and ensure a more efficient use of resources.

Environmental issues, particularly environmental legislation, affect all sizes of companies and some are more active than others in addressing these issues (Hunt and Auster, 1990). What is clear from the literature is that larger companies are more likely to have EMSs than small and medium-sized enterprises, due mainly to the availability of additional resources (Welford, 1996). They are also more likely to have formalized structures and a dedicated environmental manager to introduce and monitor their environmental management system. As a consequence, the number of organizational barriers that exist within large organizations are likely to be high and their interaction more complex.

Organizational theory

The general principles that apply to any organization offer a good basis on which to study the influence of environmental management within companies. There will be some obvious technical barriers to EMSs within the specific operations of a company, such as equipment innovations, but some of the key barriers to EMSs in an organization will be based within the non-technical organizational structure and culture of the company, as shown in Table 3.1 (Stone, 2000).

Organizational barriers

From the existing environmental management and organizational theory literature 12 organizational factors emerge that can act as barriers to EMSs. These potential organizational barriers are shown in Figure 3.1. By dissecting figure 3.1 into its key parts the various characteristics of each element can be explored. The following description of the barriers serves to support their inclusion as a potential barrier, and serves to identify the characteristics of each, enabling definition and differentiation (Eisenhardt, 1989).

Table 3.1   *Elements of an organization that can impact on the implementation of an EMS*

Elements of an Organization	Includes
The structure of the organization	Departments, subsidiaries, management hierarchy
The environment in which it operates	Geography, economic climate, legislative frameworks
The decision-making process or management of the organization	Democratic or authoritative management styles, management hierarchy
The people within the organization	Personal beliefs, priorities, level of education
The general way in which change is viewed and implemented	Management style, management hierarchy, organizational culture (proactive, reactive or passive)

Source: adapted from Stone (2000)

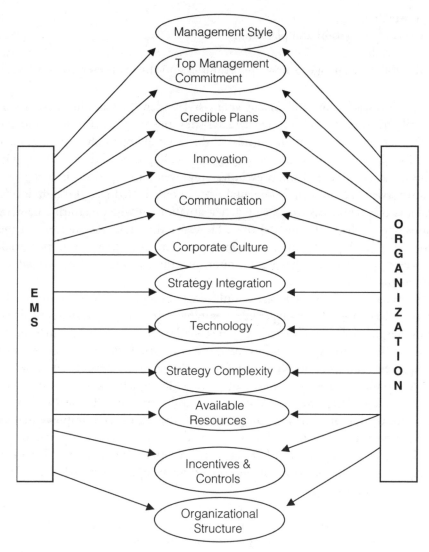

Figure 3.1   *Organizational barriers*

Management style

Companies that succeed in achieving growth and innovation in environmental performance are often those that have managers who are good at empowering employees. Management support is frequently more important to employees than a company's written commitment to environment performance because supportive behaviour from someone in a supervisory role is seen as direct encouragement (Ramus, 2002). Management style incorporates a number of factors:

- risk taking;
- levels of delegation and planning;
- teamwork;
- the ability to change as new opportunities and threats present themselves.

The various leadership and management styles identified in the literature are generally based on two opposing characteristics: the autocrat and the democrat.

Autocratic styling is often considered the classical approach to management. It is one in which the manager retains as much power and decision-making authority as possible and often excludes employee participation. It is the most effective style to adopt if environmental risk can only be reduced through detailed orders, as may be the case in an emergency situation, or when recruiting new staff to jobs with high environmental risks. However, this style of management may hinder the development of a corporate environmental plan, as it potentially excludes employees from having an input into the continuous improvement of business practices.

Democratic styling encourages employees to be a part of the decision-making process. The democratic manager keeps employees informed and shares problem-solving responsibilities. This style requires the leader to gather information and opinion from employees before making the final decision. Democratic management can produce high quality work for long periods of time and therefore is ideally suited to implementing an EMS, which is a long-term process. Many employees like the trust they receive and respond with cooperation and high morale, all of which is imperative to the continued improvement of environmental performance. However, as with the other styles, the democratic style is not always appropriate. For example, it is often more cost-effective for the manager alone to make a decision and it is an inappropriate style when employee safety is of concern.

There is no one recommended style, each has its own perceived strengths and weaknesses. Each manager is an individual made up of a mix of practical and theoretical learning experiences. The activities that occur within an organization and the level of success realized is strongly influenced by the style adopted.

Change within an organization occurs as a result of signals received from the external environment; the interpretation of these signals results in decisions being made and actions taken that change the internal aspects of an organization (Mintzberg, 1987). Different managers interpret external signals in different ways and make business decisions that suit their personality, experience and career objectives.

The ideal situation is that at the beginning of each financial year all directors and managers agree and accept the corporate objectives and the associated budgets and their reward incentives for the achievement of the objectives. This principle of overall acceptance ensures for the most part that all directors and managers have a common goal and are all moving in the same direction (Tinsley,

2002). The reality is, however, that individuals perceive objectives differently, as well as the best method for their achievement. There is a great deal of interpretation by managers and directors. Therefore new environmental strategies and systems are prioritized against other quality, safety and operational requirements leading to, at best, confusion and, at worst, obstruction (Tinsley, 2002).

Managers and directors may have accounting, marketing or engineering backgrounds and therefore respond to change in either a proactive or reactive manner. Management style is a complex concept and it is very easy to understand why it can act as a key barrier to the introduction of an EMS, particularly if used as a convenient mechanism for those corporate executives seeking a quiet, conservative life of little change (Wheeler, 1993). Even in environmentally committed companies, managers are less supportive when managing environmental activities than other business activities (Ramus, 2002) and some may even take the view that if a problem is ignored long enough it will resolve itself (Kirkland and Thompson, 1999).

A more complex view is that the traditional management concept of viewing the organization as a collection of entities or strategic business units (SBUs), competes with the growing impression that environmental management requires a holistic view of an organization (Taylor, 1992). Studies by Miller and Freisen (1980), Argyris (1993) and Pfeffer (1996) suggest that managers do not follow rational environmental practice because it falls out with their 'focus of attention'.

Managers in industries more exposed to environmental legislation and policies must first translate these legislative and policy requirements into achievable objectives before implementing cost-effective operational strategies (Currie, 1993).

Key managerial behaviour for the implementation of improved environmental performance

Ramus (2002) outlines six managerial behaviours that improve environmental performance, ranking them according to their strongest impact, as shown in Table 3.2.

Top management commitment

Early environmental management systems were generally isolated from the main function of the organization (Shelton, 1994). This was in part due to the failure of top management who expected environmental management to adapt to the prevailing business culture, and in part to environmental managers who expected to be accepted into the organization (Hunt and Auster, 1990; Buzzelli, 1991). Cohen and Levinthal (1990) referred to this phenomenon as an organization's 'absorptive capacity'.

Table 3.2   *Key managerial behaviours*

Managerial Behaviour	Comments
Environmental communication	• Democratic management style show that managers are willing to listen to employees' environmental ideas, which encourages creativity and participation.
	• A non-hierarchical approach encourages employees to communicate directly with other business areas to solve problems.
Environmental competence building	• Provides environmental problem-solving tools. • Supports employee eco-innovation.
	• Managers should be trained in environmental sustainability so that they are able to support employees and to ensure that they understand the benefit of giving employees the time and resources to commit to environmental improvements.
Environmental rewards and recognition	• Environmental awards, bonus pay, regular feedback and praise all encourage employees to improve environmental performance.
Management of environmental goals and responsibilities	• Delegating responsibility to individuals and setting of targets directly correlate to improvements in employee environmental performance rates.
Environmental innovation	• Managers who are open to new ideas and have an innovative and experimental approach to problem solving encourage others to innovate.
Dissemination	• Employee perception of a company's commitment to a written environmental policy has important impacts on environmental actions.
	• Continuous dissemination leads to continuous motivation towards environmental performance.
	• Dissemination is often considered the least important because managers are generally poor at disseminating information.

Source: adapted from Ramus (2002)

Absorptive capacity is seen as a function of an organization's prior related knowledge. That is, an organization's capacity for assimilating and applying external information for commercial benefit. In the case of environmental management, the absorptive capacity theory would imply that prior knowledge is limited and therefore the introduction of an EMS would be difficult because the lack of top management knowledge could limit the level of commitment (Kirkland and Thompson, 1999).

The difficulty for senior management is that once an investment decision has been made, they rely on feedback information to determine whether the investment decision was a correct one. Often any negative feedback received before the investment objective has been realized can have a detrimental effect on continued commitment. Once uncertainty has been created over an investment decision, senior management commitment can wane, particularly when additional resource requirements are no longer viewed as investment but as expense (Cohen and Levinthal, 1990). It is at this point that decision making slows and more analysis is required before further resources are committed. The final outcome may be that investment decisions stall or are abandoned completely (Shelton, 1994).

Credible plans

Inappropriate or 'quick fix' plans to introduce an EMS to an organization are a risky strategy (Kirkland and Thompson, 1999). Instead, the use of credible, well formulated plans can benefit the organization in two main areas. First, environmental issues can pose complex problems for organizations, therefore the plans created must highlight and address the complexity by reducing it to its simplest form. Second, credible plans reduce the potential for management mistakes that can quickly lead to disenchantment and loss of credibility, creating general resistance to the introduction of the EMSs.

Good planning that is based on good analysis of good data can have many EMS benefits:

- increasing general awareness;
- reducing risk in decision making;
- identifying aspects and impacts of products, processes and services;
- establishing agreement on organizational priorities.

The key difficulty in formulating credible plans is ensuring that associated policy statements, procedures, plans and budgets are coordinated.

Innovation

Innovation has been identified as causing delays, obstruction, misunderstandings and disagreements in newly installed organizational systems (Irwin et al, 1994; Roome, 1994). Innovation, or the lack of it, is also an issue in the implementation of environmental management systems. Porter and van der Linde's (1995) study suggests that too many companies spend too many environmental pounds on fighting regulation and stalling legislation when they should be finding real environmental solutions to environmental issues.

Such factors as consumer demand, government influence and legislation impact on the rate, scale and type of industrial innovation within organizations (Foster and Green, 2000). As a consequence, the development of a new or even modified environmental product can take up a lot of time and scarce resources before it becomes part of an organization's product portfolio.

The organizational decision-making process for the acceptance of promising environmental innovation can also be biased. Exploring the use of innovation in environmental management, Cramer and Zegveld (1991) found that the innovations that were eventually selected appeared to be the most successful or advantageous in a competitive, rather than environmental, development sense.

Rennings et al (forthcoming) divide innovation into three types:

1   Process innovations that enable the production of greater output with the same or lesser input.
2   Product innovation that improves goods or services, or leads to the development of new products.
3   Organizational innovation that refers to new forms of management.

Environmental innovation can similarly be divided into two types:

1   Innovations in end-of-pipe technologies – usually add-on measures that allow a piece of equipment to comply with legislation, such as filters, sound absorbers and sewage treatments.
2   Innovation in integrated technologies – modifications or new equipment for cleaner production to remove the harmful by-products at source throughout the process.

The process of innovation can be undertaken with small steps or giant strides, but whatever method is selected, barriers can arise. A slow incremental approach gives a signal of low priority and provides competitors with time to deliver similar or alternative products or services. A radical approach can create a force-field of resistance through competition for resources, lack of adequate planning and lack of understanding of product marketing and manufacturing requirements. The company must meet the costs of innovation, which cannot always be recuperated through effective marketing, particularly if competitors are able to respond quickly by copying the improvements (Rennings et al, forthcoming).

Manager and employee role in innovation

Employee creativity has a role to play in innovation; it is an important problem-solving resource in a company. However, in order to use this resource, companies must provide the systems with which to support employee action, and managers often do not give the same level of support to employee environmental activities as general management tasks (Ramus, 2002).

A study conducted by Ramus (2002) identified that it is the role of environmental policy to show employees that the company desires environmental ideas or actions, but that this needs to be supported by direct encouragement from supervisors and managers.

Ramus (2002) splits employee eco-innovation into three types:

1   those that decrease the environmental impacts of the company;
2   those that solve a particular environmental problem for the company;
3   those that develop a more eco-efficient product or service.

Communications

Fuller and Swanson (1992) and Azzone and Bertelè (1994) suggest that a lack of education and communication can act as barriers, particularly if not diffused successfully throughout the organization. While a number of organizations are attempting to introduce EMSs, often those managers tasked with the responsibility of introducing the systems lack the necessary training and education (Kirkland and Thompson, 1999). Managers who have the required levels of education and training know the importance of raising levels of environmental knowledge among other employees.

With change, the existing behaviour patterns and values of an organization are often questioned. Individuals can feel threatened, particularly if there is a lack of communication to aid understanding of the new organizational direction and the new roles of its employees. The use of departmental briefings, organizational seminars, work groups, intranet and newsletters are useful formal methods of communicating change. Informal communication methods such as 'corridor briefings' or 'canteen chat' can also be useful.

The best option can often be a mix of both the formal and informal as long as a consistent message is being communicated. Whatever communication methods are used, if change is to be managed successfully then the communication process needs to be two-way. Senior management must not be perceived as having all the answers and delivering directives to middle managers. Presenting the problem to middle managers to solve can be very rewarding, not just for the managers but also for the successful implementation of the new EMS (Tinsley, 2001).

Another way in which communication can be a barrier is if a company does not cultivate every possible means to communicate with their customers, for instance through newsletters, websites and environmental reports, to let their customers know that they are environmentally aware. The implementation of an EMS is accepted as an image-builder to strengthen a company's competitive position (Hui et al, 2001), but this competitive advantage can only be realized if customer communication is effective.

In 1998 a study was undertaken to explore environmental communication at EMI Music (Ramus, 1998). The study highlighted some ways in which communication could be improved:

- Continual reiteration of the company's overall environmental vision by the senior managers.
- Involvement of all staff in environmental programmes.
- Annual updating of environmental policies, manuals and the environmental reports, which should be distributed to all staff.
- Adopting both top-down and bottom-up communication of environmental information through meetings, electronic media and suggestion boxes.
- Employee surveys to assess the effectiveness of the environmental communication system.
- Accreditation certificates and awards campaigns to keep employees aware of goals and target achievement.

Corporate culture

A company's culture can be defined by the prevailing values and attitudes that stem from previously adopted problem-solving approaches to environmental management issues (Welford and Gouldson, 1993). Due to the speed, range and complexity of environmental issues, organizations need to internalize and operationalize policies and programmes to be consistent with long-term goals (Corbett and Wassenhove, 1993). Shimell (1991) argues that culture change produces long-term business benefits to the likes of 3M and Dow Chemical (see Box 1.2). Previous cosmetic or public relation responses to environmental issues have proved to be ineffective and have at times back-fired on organizations (Peattie, 1990).

Organizational culture reflects the way people perform tasks, set objectives, administer resources and the way they feel and respond to daily opportunities and threats. Culture is so fundamental to the way an organization works that people respond in an unconscious manner to a way of working within it. The prevailing culture is the driving force for the whole organization.

Stone (2000) lists elements of a company's culture that are relevant to the uptake of cleaner technologies and identifies the importance of the human dimension to the successful implementation of environmental improvement. Three key elements are discussed in more detail below:

- commitment of decision makers and style of management;
- encouragement and training of staff;
- strategic attitude.

Commitment of decision makers and style of management

Both commitment of senior management and management style have been already discussed, but both are key to the culture of the organization. Whatever style leads the organization, the culture will be created through the initial setting of objectives. The setting of policies, structure, control and reward systems to achieve the objectives will also reflect the culture (Mintzberg, 1987).

Encouragement and training of staff

Companies that show trust in their employees to act responsibly tend to be successful in implementing a culture conducive to environmental improvements. Employees should be encouraged to take ownership of the processes that they are involved in and also look outside of their own job responsibilities (Ramus, 1998). It has been stated that competitive advantage derived from environmental improvement will be found in those companies that empower staff by making use of their ability to learn and giving them the tools with which to apply this learning to all areas of the business (Hutchinson, 1996). A lack of specialist knowledge stemming from an absence of training outside the remit of the main job is a barrier to reaching environmental goals (Ramus, 1998).

Environmental training may be incorporated into all levels of existing training programmes within a company, or specific environmental programmes may be offered. Some organizations offer external environmental educational opportunities, such as job rotation and site visits. However, supervisory encouragement still remains a key factor in the success of any type of employee training (Ramus, 2002).

Strategic attitude

A key part of an organization's culture that will impact on its EMS success is strategic attitude, also referred to as management approaches. Azzone et al (1997) highlight three key strategies that organizations may follow when positioning themselves to meet competitive challenges:

1   *Compliance-based attitude*: a company takes action only according to external pressure from competitors or the wider market.
2   *Anticipatory attitude*: while reacting to external pressures, a company anticipates future changes and implements proactive initiatives.
3   *Innovative attitudes*: a company implements changes in management procedures to introduce a new product to an existing market, therefore creating a breakthrough in product performance.

Clearly from these categories the more passive approaches are going to lead to a less proactive pursuit of EMSs. Ironically, a compliance-based attitude could work more effectively if it already has an EMS in place, as it could react more rapidly to external pressures as and when they occur.

For the two more active attitude categories that are more likely to implement EMSs, the structured framework of an EMS will aid the anticipatory attitude to recognize future change, and the innovative attitude will quickly be able to identify key procedures or processes that are candidates for innovation.

Other authors have categorized management approaches in similar ways, all based on the proactive stance of the attitude, for example Vastag et al (1996) list four approaches: reactive, proactive, strategic and crisis prevention. The categorization of companies according to their attitude and circumstances is a useful tool for academics to study effectiveness of EMSs. These categorization models are discussed in more detail in Chapter 4.

System integration

The literature suggests that it is the system itself, its complexity (Roome, 1992; Rothenberg et al, 1992; Avila and Whitehead, 1993), its level of integration (Punjari and Wright, 1994; Shelton, 1994; Welford, 1996) and its 'fit' with the existing organizational structure (Prothero and McDonagh, 1992) and culture (Peattie, 1990; Beaumont, 1992; Corbett and Wassenhove, 1993; Shrivastava and Hart, 1994) that determine the success of an EMS.

The main difficulty for managers is that 'one size does not fit all' when it comes to implementing a successful system. Each organization is different in terms of its culture and the way it undertakes its business activities. Any new environmental system must fit with the prevailing political, operational and economic needs of each organization (Rothenberg et al 1992). In addition, some managers may take the view that the issue of system complexity is compounded when environmental, quality and health and safety systems are integrated as one system (Tinsley, 2002).

Technology

Technology in this context may be used to describe the hardware (machinery) and software (systems and techniques) used to process and present data in a meaningful form, or used to describe the hardware used as part of the business, such as in manufacturing. In the first case, it has been argued that because of the complexity of information involved, flows of information tend to be more upward than downward (Lorsch and Allen, 1973). Another barrier may occur as a result of managers selecting and preferring personal contact and informal communication to assist with network development and decision making. A key issue for decision makers is how to react to information received from a source that is viewed sceptically and not trusted and that uses an unfamiliar language.

In the case of technologies used within the business (for example factory machines or printing presses) environmentally sound technologies are those that ensure efficient resource use with reduced wastage and emissions. Many environmental problems within a business may centre on the inefficiencies of technology choice. While innovations and technology improvements are continually being made, new technologies often require new skills and training and broader infrastructure support in terms of management and maintenance (Hale, 1995). All these things come at a cost of time and finance, and often companies may be dissuaded from upgrading or modifying equipment because the initial cost cannot be regained quickly enough.

Strategy complexity

The more complex the strategy, the more friction is created between strategy formulation and strategy implementation. Senior management may perceive the unsuccessful implementation of new strategies to be the fault of middle management, seen as being either unsupportive or ill-informed of the new direction. Middle managers consider that new strategies tend to be successful if there are a clear set of strategy objectives and priorities and a shared level of understanding and commitment (Floyd and Wooldridge, 1992).

Rothenberg et al (1992) found that effective environmental strategies were integrated with existing corporate strategies that were consistent with organizational characteristics and operating context. The purpose of an EMS is to make complex environmental issues manageable (Kirkland and Thompson, 1999), but unfortunately, managers and other stakeholders are prone to see environmental management systems as adding to the existing organizational complexity they have to deal with.

The larger the organization, the more substructures become a consideration when implementing an environmental strategy. Many organizational groups or strategic business units may have their own set of goals, time perspectives and decision-making processes. Designing strategies without consideration of these substructures and their respective strengths and weaknesses may hinder the implementation process (Rothenberg et al, 1992). The recognition of different substructures within an organization may lead to a more effective route to environmental strategic change and lead to the identification of additional product or service development opportunities.

Available resources

The introduction of an EMS may be hampered by the shortage of adequate resources or by the lack of recognition or provision of necessary resources (Greeno and Robinson, 1992). The lack of available budgets, human resources and corporate incentives (Gallarotti, 1995; Tapon and Sarabura, 1995) are identified as potential barriers. A lack of resources or the misallocation of resources may result from other existing barriers, such as limited commitment or poor communication (Kirkland and Thompson, 1999). A study by Tinsley and Melton (1997) highlighted the problem of low prioritization of resources for addressing environmental issues when faced with daily operational requirements.

Incentives and controls

Environmental systems and programmes cannot be introduced into organizations through senior management directives; incentives and controls must be in place to ensure employee support. Tapon and Sarabura (1995) suggest that full employee involvement through group learning situations is more beneficial to an organization than relying on solutions from experts. Dow Chemical's 'Waste Reduction Always Pays' programme is one example of an incentive scheme that rewards employees with generous financial incentives for environmental improvement. Compaq/Hewlett Packard require managers and directors to agree to environmental objectives, together with budgets and incentive schemes to ensure the realization of the set objectives (Tinsley, 2002).

Organizational structure

Organizational structure is a framework that allows corporate strategy to be pursued. The relationship between strategy and structure is important if an organization is to successfully achieve its corporate objectives (Miles and Snow, 1978). An organization will, however, adopt a structure that best meets the demands of a unique set of internal and external pressures.

The cross-disciplinary, cross-functional nature of environmental issues leads Roome (1994) to suggest that organizations need to reform their existing structure. The development of an environmentally successful company requires problems of environmental inertia to be addressed, which are familiar in organizations striving to move from one set of structures, systems and values to new frameworks (Mintzberg, 1987).

The importance of this point is underlined in Punjari and Wright's (1994) study that also finds that there cannot be an effective EMS without a change of structure or organization. A change in an organization's structure or strategy usually takes the form of planners presenting plans to top management for acceptance and resourcing (Piercy, 1989). Piercy suggests that barriers are created when the plans for change are accepted and attention is then turned to the issue of implementation. He states that at this juncture top management considerably underestimate the costs and problems of getting the new plans accepted.

Additionally, it can be argued that directors and managers have a choice of whether to adapt to or resist organizational change. Those who prefer the process of adaptation would modify existing corporate strategies to better match those changes that are occurring externally (Child, 1972). Those directors and managers inclined to preserve existing strategies would be reluctant to change in response to external pressure.

BARRIERS IN SMALL TO MEDIUM ENTERPRISES

In the case of SMEs the barriers highlighted in this chapter take on a different emphasis due to the particular structure of the smaller enterprise. In a smaller company the investment of resources needed to implement an EMS is more significant when compared to the overall turnover of the business, but potential improvements are also more significant to the future success of the business.

Hillary (2004) performed a study of SMEs to determine the benefits and drawbacks to SMEs of implementing EMSs. Three main benefits rising were identified:

1 *Commercial benefits* – attraction of new business and customers and the satisfaction of customer requirements.
2 *Environmental benefits* – assured legal compliance, energy and material efficiency and reductions in energy consumption and waste production.
3 *Communication* – enhanced image and better dialogue with stakeholders.

However, while these benefits are significant to any business, many SMEs find the barriers to implementing EMSs so great that these benefits cannot be realized. Some of the barriers are listed in Table 3.3.

The barriers discussed in this chapter can reduce the impact of an EMS or make it unsustainable, but rarely does any individual barrier stop an EMS from being implemented within the larger companies. Some of the barriers identified by

Table 3.3 *Barriers for small to medium enterprises*

Resources	• Few SMEs can afford to employ full-time environmental managers so that the demands of the EMS implementation take managers away from their main job responsibilities
	• The multifunctional role of staff undertaking an EMS along with their usual jobs means that employees may not have the time to give either responsibility the required attention
	• Few general managers have the technical knowledge to implement an EMS or the time to improve their knowledge
	• The high cost of certification and verification disproportionally penalizes smaller companies
	• Underestimation of resource requirements leads to SMEs giving up before they achieve any benefits

Table 3.3   *Barriers for small to medium enterprises* (cont'd)

Understanding and perception	• Lack of awareness of benefits may reduce company motivation for implementing an EMS
	• Lack of understanding may reduce the value of environmental reporting therefore leading to ineffective communication with stakeholders
	• Perceived high cost of implementation and maintenance
	• Uncertainty about the commercial market value of EMSs
Implementation	• Implementation can be interrupted, which lengthens the process and can lead to waning interest in completion
	• Inability to see the relevance of all the stages
Lack of rewards	• SMEs found that components of the EMS failed to meet expectations, such as automatic compliance with regulations, competitive advantage and stakeholder satisfaction
Attitudes and company culture	• Management instability
	• Potential low status of the person leading the EMS implementation
	• Resistance to change
	• Lack of internal marketing of the EMS
Support and guidance	• Lack of accessible financial assistance
	• Lack of consultants with experience in implementing EMSs in SMEs
	• Inconsistent approach of consultants to EMS implementation
	• Lack of sector specific exemplars
	• Lack of trade association or network of support
	• Poor quality information of conflicting guidance
EMS surprises	• SMEs often underestimate the resources required to implement an EMS and are unable to rectify the situation with further resources due to the scale of the company

Source: modified from Hillary (2002)

Hillary (2004), such as lack of assistance, underestimating resource requirements and additional demands on existing staff to the detriment of the business, often stop EMS implementation at the first stage within small to medium enterprises, so that no proper attempt to implement an EMS is ever made.

4

Models for Classifying Environmental Management Strategies

INTRODUCTION

While an EMS provides a framework for implementing environmental improvements, the unique mixture of drivers and barriers within each company means that each must have their own environmental strategy, integrating business needs and environmental needs, into realistic objectives and targets. This chapter explores strategy adoption together with the models that academics use to compare and contrast the effectiveness of the different approaches to continued environmental improvement.

BACKGROUND

Environmental management systems offer a framework and accreditation system for organizations to use in creating continued environmental improvements. However, in reality each EMS must adapt to the business environment (Greeno and Robinson, 1992) and so a standardized EMS will need some modifications if implementation is to be successful. Companies can have any combination of drivers (as discussed in Chapter 1) for implementing EMSs (Azzone et al, 1997). With different drivers towards EMSs, the strategies adopted to achieve environmental improvement will also differ so that no single strategy will suit every organization. In addition to this, as seen in Chapter 3, the specific barriers present in a company will also determine the route that the organization takes towards its EMS and if full accreditation is ever achieved. Companies often make mistakes by employing regulatory experts or consultants who impose common guidelines on companies that do not have the same needs or do not operate under the same social and economic constraints (Vastag et al, 1996).

While the standardized ISO 14000 series was not introduced until 1996, before this year many companies had set up their own environmental procedures that worked so efficiently that there was no requirement to change to the standardized system. For this reason, standardization is yet to be achieved and there remain a large variety of different procedures and strategies adopted by companies all over the world. Such variation suggests that there are many ways in which environmental behaviour can be successful (Azzone et al, 1997; Khanna and Anton, 2002) but has made it very difficult for academics to study the benefits and drawbacks of environmental strategies.

TYPES OF ENVIRONMENTAL STRATEGY

Companies adopt very different 'green' strategies according to their attitude to environmental issues; some choosing to go no further than what is required of them, others to go beyond compliance to ensure they are leaders in their market.

For some companies, environmentalism is considered a threat and strategies are only implemented when required by environmental regulations. A survey of 85 companies in the United States showed that 50 per cent of them were focusing narrowly on compliance (Azzone et al, 1997). Other companies initiate voluntary transformation in environmental management to ensure continued improvement as they consider the environment as a competitive priority (González-Benito and González-Benito, 2005). This is the case, for instance, in 3M, which has introduced aggressive product development strategies aimed at avoiding the use of solvents in its products (see Box 1.2). In addition, some companies adopt green strategies to gain credibility with local communities and government agencies, even though this may not achieve any benefits in terms of product acceptance (Azzone et al, 1997).

While the sustainability of different environmental strategies can be reliant on the available resources and the employees' green competencies, as discussed in Chapter 3, the company's environmental culture and its strategic attitude are also key factors.

Environmental strategies have been classified by Azzone et al (1997) and are listed below. They are based around the attitudes of companies discussed in Chapter 3 that can act as barriers to EMSs:

- *Passive, lobbying-based environmental strategy.* Companies with a compliance-based attitude that try to influence governments, regulators and customers to delay the implementation of new regulations of the development of new markets. These companies see environmental improvements as a threat rather than an opportunity.
- *Reactive environmental strategy.* Reacting to external pressure from 'green movements', governments, regulators and other firms outside the sector whose initiatives could be successfully transferred.
- *Anticipatory green strategy.* Carefully considered timing of environmental initiatives providing competitive advantage for the future. Strategies include the early development of technology for the long-term saving of resources.

- *Innovation-based green strategy.* Where the environment is seen as the most important competitive priority and innovation is used as a solution to improve environmental performance and fulfil new market needs with environmentally friendly products.

The anticipatory and innovation-based strategies are those that belong to the most proactive companies, and proactive companies are those companies that have the greatest opportunity to benefit from EMSs in the broadest range of ways including the more elusive competitive advantage (Morrow and Rondinelli, 2002). Ramus (2002) identifies key environmental policies that exist in environmentally proactive companies:

- A written environmental policy including specific targets for the improvements of environmental performance.
- Publication of an environmental report.
- An environmental management system.
- Green purchasing policy, including the reduction of unsustainable products.
- Environmental training for all employees.
- Employee responsibility for environmental performance.
- Life-cycle analysis policy.
- Management understanding of sustainable development.
- Fossil fuel reduction policy.
- Toxic chemical use reduction policy.
- Using the same environmental standards abroad as at home.

STUDYING ENVIRONMENTAL MANAGEMENT USING COMPARATIVE MODELS

In an attempt to improve understanding of environmental management, academics and practitioners have sought to classify corporate environmental behaviour and evaluate performance (Kolk and Mauser, 2002). To this end many models have been constructed to identify patterns for improved performance or competitive advantage. Environmental management models first emerged in 1987 (Petulla, 1987). The models were used based on traditional classification and categorical techniques to understand social and organizational phenomena. Despite criticisms of inflexibility, environmental models have been considered useful in understanding organizational structures and strategies in an environmental context. Since 1987 over 50 environmental management models have been created (Kolk and Mauser, 2002). They generally fall into two main categories: typology and continuum. Typology models categorize on the basis of a company's current situation, while continuum models categorize according to a progression towards environmental excellence.

Typology models

A typology consists of a conceptually derived interrelated set of ideal types. Some of the environmental models created attempt to categorize an organization's position in relation to its current environmental situation. Unlike continuum models there is no set of criteria used for categorizing organizations into mutually exclusive groups. The organization is classified by the way it addresses environmental issues at one moment in time and there is no attempt to identify future environmental development or response options. Examples of some of these models are listed in Table 4.1 with a brief overview of the categories used.

Continuum models

A continuum is a linear classification scheme that identifies a continuous, not discrete, structure in time. Continuum models are classification schemes that characterize phenomena into mutually exclusive groups. Each company can be identified using set criteria that position it within a particular stage or phase on a developmental scale or continuum. Examples of continuum models are given in Table 4.2, with a good example of a continuum model being Hunt and Auster's (1990) five-stage model.

Key models

This chapter centres around five models:

1   Typology: Greening Model (Winn and Angell, 2000).
2   Typology: Classification of environmental policies (Vastag et al, 1996).
3   Continuum: Environmental Contexts (Azzone and Bertelè, 1994).

Table 4.1   *Examples of typology models*

Name	Model Title	Categories
Steger (1988)	Environmental strategies	Indifferent, defensive, offensive, innovative
Lee and Green (1994)	Strategic options for green product development	Do nothing, generic strategies, diversification, remedy, tonic, bread and butter, nimble, leadership, pioneer
Vastag et al (1996)	Classification of environmental policies	Reactive, proactive, crisis preventative, strategic
Winn and Angell (2000)	Corporate greening	Deliberate reactive greening, unrealized greening, emergent active greening, deliberate proactive greening

Table 4.2   *Examples of continuum models*

Name	Model Title	Categories/Stages
Hunt and Auster (1990)	Stages of Environmental Management	Beginner, fire-fighter, concerned citizen, pragmatist, proactivist
Greeno (1991)	Posture towards environmental issues	Problem solving, managing for compliance, managing for assurance
Müller and Koechlin (1992)	Stages of Environmental Strategy	Ostriches, Chicken Lickens, Green Hornets, Robin Hood
Roome (1992)	Strategic option responses to environmental pressures	Non-compliance, compliance, compliance plus, commercial and environmental excellence, leading edge
Azzone and Bertelè (1994)	Environmental contexts	Stable, reactive, anticipatory, proactive, creative
Dodge and Welford (1995)	ROAST Scale	Resistance, observe and comply, accommodate, seize and pre-empt, transcend
Hart (1997)	Environmental strategy	Pollution prevention, product stewardship, clean technology

4   Continuum: Strategic Options Model (Roome, 1992).
5   Continuum: Five-Stage Model (Hunt and Auster, 1990).

Greening model
Winn and Angell (2000) build a 'greening' model on observations made while studying a variety of companies. The categories describe the attitude of companies towards 'greening'.

Deliberate reactive greening
Companies that undergo 'deliberate reactive' greening engage in specific environmental activities only when forced to do so by regulatory authorities. They have a weak top management commitment to the environment; the environment is not seen as the company's responsibility. Environmental considerations are not considered part of functional or operational decision making. No monitoring activities are performed and performance is never measured so that new regulation or emerging environmental issues may often come as a surprise to the company.

Unrealized greening
Companies that undergo 'unrealized' greening have a lack of formal planning and monitoring, leaving the company often unable to cope with new developments

in legislation. These companies may have environmental policies that consider the environment in decision making and top management commitment, but they do not have a proactive approach to implementation and do not include environmental considerations in their organizational goals. There is very little environmental innovation and product design is not executed with the environment in mind.

Emergent active greening

Companies that undergo 'emergent active' greening perceive opportunities from environmental activities, such as cost savings, and have a proactive approach to environmental activity up to a middle management level. These companies take responsibility for the environment through 'green' product design and the company monitors its own environmental performance and engages in planning and external monitoring activities with prevention of environmental problems in mind. The company generates environmental product innovations but the environment is not systematically considered in all decisions across all functions and no management commitment is shown above middle management level.

Deliberate proactive greening

Companies that follow 'deliberate proactive' greening have a systematic approach to environmental activities. They put environmental commitment and implementation high on their agenda and are environmental innovators. The environment is a consideration in all functional decisions and material flows analysis is a tool that is used to design products with the environment in mind. Top management is committed to the environment and to sustainable development and these companies are capable of preventing environmental problems by using systems to plan, monitor and anticipate.

Classification of environmental policies

Vastag et al (1996) classify environmental management approaches so as to group companies into differing typologies. The classifications consist of groups A to D: reactive, proactive, strategic and crisis prevention.

Group A, reactive environmental management

This group refers to industries that have low environmental emissions, which do not confer a great risk and are unlikely to affect a great number of people. This group also contains companies that use non-exhaustible resources, little energy and limited transportation. Typically, industries that use well developed technologies, such as textiles and food producers may successfully exist within this group as environmental management simply calls for regulatory compliance rather than the development of environmental contingency plans in the event of an accident. In this way, the responsibility for environmental compliance can safely remain with the existing middle management.

Group B, proactive environmental management

This group refers to those industries with technologies that create high levels of environmentally harmful pollution, but due to their location and a good environmental infrastructure they can significantly reduce adverse effects to a minimum. However, in order to reduce the potential environmental risks, managers need to anticipate changes in legislation, technology and customer opinion. In this group, environmental management tends to be decentralized and concentrated at the source of the environmental risk, for example manufacturing plants.

Group C, strategic environmental management

This group consists of highly polluting industries that operate in a context that increases risk through external conditions, such as the public's attitude. Chemical companies that are based within city boundaries are included in this group. Under these circumstances, environmental management should be implemented right up to senior management level. These companies are often involved in initiatives that go beyond compliance and have an aggressive approach to preventing environmental damage. Environmental strategies must be well defined, well communicated and well monitored.

Group D, crisis preventive environmental management

This group does not contain great polluters due to the small volumes of resources they use or because pollution is indirectly made. Examples of these industries include the tourism industry, electric energy plants and fast food chains. However, any pollution that is directly created will affect large numbers of people. A crisis prevention approach is therefore best suited; the occurrence of environmental impacts is small but far-reaching. Environmental strategies include a mixture of improving technological procedures to reduce risk and educational campaigns to ensure that the public does not misperceive the dangers in the event of pollution.

Environmental contexts

Azzone and Bertelè (1994) suggest that an organization may adopt one of five environmental contexts: stable, reactive, anticipative, proactive and creative. A stable context results in management having a lack of awareness of the organization's impact upon the environment. Organizations in a reactive context merely respond to environmental problems and environmentalism evolves slowly. An anticipative context occurs through strong public awareness and pressure that speed environmental change. The proactive context is characterized by the drive for environmental change through available technology, while a creative context is the search for technology that will aid environmental improvement.

Stable
Environmental legislation has extremely limited consequences for the companies due to the nature of the business so that the frequency of introducing a new standard is very low. This is more often the result of a lack of perception of environmental problems within the company, coupled with a lack of obvious environmental implications due to the nature of the business and lack of customer demand for environmental performance.

Reactive
Attention to environmental problems is limited to those who work within hazardous conditions and so environmental legislation is taken up slowly as and when required; adherence to legislation is considered an operational problem.

Anticipative
This includes companies that have more environmentally-minded customers, and therefore must meet more demanding standards. Environmental issues become the source of technological innovation usually as a way of meeting more demanding industry standards, particularly for companies based in the European Union. Innovation is therefore more process based than product based.

Proactive
Green consumerism has an ever stronger influence, and innovation is more product based than process based. This includes smaller niche markets, such as the detergent industry, but is growing due to the continuous growth of green consumerism.

Creative
This is best characterized by sectors such as the plastics industry where the general public is aware of the environmental problems associated with the industry, but the best ways forward cannot be agreed upon. Technology is generally agreed to be the best solution, but even the best solutions have their drawbacks (for example with the plastics industry, recycling is often not energy efficient and biodegradable plastics produce toxic by-products).

Strategic Options Model
Roome's (1992) Strategic Options Model suggests that organizations have five broad theoretical options: non-compliance, compliance, compliance plus,

commercial and environmental excellence, and leading edge. These classifications are based on how an organization reacts to environmental legislation and public and corporate pressures.

Non-compliance

This strategy is one of default, whether through competing objectives, lack of managerial vision or cost constraints on an organization. Taken consciously or unconsciously, this strategy is a choice not to incorporate environmental imperatives.

Compliance

Reacting to environmental legislative requirements is a compliance strategy. As legislation lags environmental problems so the organization adopting this strategy could be considered to be backward thinking and unaware of future environmental developments that may provide a competitive advantage through new marketing or waste and energy efficiency opportunities.

Compliance plus

Here Roome (1994) classifies those organizations that take a proactive position on environmental management as having a compliance plus strategy. Developing such a strategy requires that environmental management systems are integrated into an organization's business strategy framework. According to Roome (1994) the key difference between a compliance and compliance plus strategy is for management to move from a reactive to proactive management style. Such a movement would require the involvement of senior management to challenge existing management strategies and promote organizational change.

Excellence

Roome (1994) identifies strategies four and five with the fourth strategy awarding commercial and environmental excellence where organizations use the best business, quality and management strategies to demonstrate good management practice. He classifies the fifth strategy as leading edge. Organizations using this strategy signal a specific or specialized form of practice. Those organizations adopting this strategy are applying leading-edge thinking in environmental management and generally set the standards for other organizations to follow.

The importance of Roome's (1994) study is that he identifies the need for organizational change to ensure the acceptance of an environmental management system. He recognizes the need for planned programmed change to move compliant organizations to compliance plus or excellence organizations. He argues that compliance strategies are based on clean technology techniques such as waste minimization and energy efficiency and are built around the requirements of environmental legislation or regulation.

The five-stage model

One of the earlier continuum studies on the development stages of environmental management was undertaken in 1990 by Hunt and Auster. They investigated how organizations managed pollution control and reduced exposure to environmental risk. During the course of their study they found that organizations were spread along an environmental developmental continuum. At the lower end of the continuum organizations were found to have either no environmental management strategies or strategies that were so constrained by the lack of resources or operations they were rendered largely ineffectual.

Hunt and Auster's (1990) five-stage model suggests that each stage of environmental development represents a generic characteristic, and the specific requirements of each will vary according to the type of business, the range of potential environmental problems, the size of the organization and the complexity of the corporate structure. Of all the models identified, Hunt and Auster's (1990) model would provide a strong basis from which to determine an organization's stage of environmental development.

The models discussed in greater detail in this chapter focus, for the most part, on the external factors that effect organizational change and identify the external pressures that influence the type of EMS being introduced into an organization. Hunt and Auster's (1990) model, by contrast, explores the five stages of organizational internal environmental development.

The five corporate environmental developmental stages of Hunt and Auster's findings are worthy of exploration in greater detail.

Stage 1, the beginner

At the lower end of the continuum, organizations without environmental management strategies are classified as beginners. Organizations whose strategies are based upon extending a senior engineer's or operational manager's responsibilities to include environmental management are also classed as beginners. Those organizations, such as banks, insurance companies and similar service focused organizations that see themselves as having no impact upon the environment are also included as beginners.

According to Hunt and Auster's classification, when a beginner, corporate managers consider environmental management to be unnecessary and top management support and resource commitment is minimal at best. Stage 1 offers no solution to an organization seeking to reduce its exposure to environmental risk.

Stage 2, the fire-fighter

The second stage of the five-stage model identifies the fire-fighter. Organizations at this stage of environmental development are focused on fire-fighting as a reactive approach by management, whose strategy is one of resolving environmental problems as and when they occur. Generally, organizations with this kind of strategy rely on a small environmental team to address environmental issues as they occur and prioritize on the basis of immediate risk. Such a strategy tends to emerge from the allocation of minimal resources and due to the necessity to prioritize environmental issues; the organization remains open to serious environmental risk from those problems that have yet to surface.

Stage 3, the concerned citizen

Those organizations aware that environmental issues are part of business activities take a compliance stance and use environmental specialists to identify and address potential areas of environmental risk. Organizations adopting the strategy of the concerned citizen are aware of their environmental regulatory and legislative responsibilities and ensure sufficient resources are made available to monitor and report on the likelihood of environmental risk.

Stage 4, the pragmatist

At the pragmatic stage companies are no longer reacting to environmental problems but are taking time to plan and manage the activities that reduce the likelihood of a problem arising. The environmental department of the pragmatic company is well equipped with skilled personnel, has sufficient resources and the authority to ensure effective operation.

In Hunt and Auster's model companies achieving stage four are considered to be very organized and efficient in reducing environmental risk. There are good recording, monitoring and auditing systems in place to support the operation of an EMS. Despite these achievements it is argued that even at stage four, environmental management is still not a top priority. There remains a risk at this stage that funding for environmental development may be tenuous and the impact of the environmental team over operational necessity is limited. Hunt and Auster considered that those companies with such a pragmatic approach to environmental management are those that are in industry sectors such as the petrochemical and manufacturing sectors, attracting intense scrutiny from regulatory bodies and environmental action groups.

Stage 5, the proactivist

At the 'proactivist' stage there are strong links between management and corporate environmental goals and objectives. The people involved are knowledgeable, motivated and high-profile individuals who take the concept of environmental management beyond policing and prevention. Environmental training and awareness programmes are supported and encouraged at all levels of management. There is a strong link between the environmental function and senior management assisted by direct reporting relationships, formal and informal meetings, and networks. Environmental management is a top priority for this type of organization and it is supported by committed directors and a strong budget. Hunt and Auster's model is similar to that of Roome's (1992) Strategic Options Model where Roome also classifies organizations into those that do not comply, those that comply and those that exceed their environmental responsibilities.

AN INTEGRATED APPROACH

Traditionally, environmental management strategies within organizations have been compliance oriented. To comply with environmental legislative requirements, organizations established small environmental units to deal with legislative and regulatory requirements. As a consequence, these environmental units failed to be sufficiently effective. The environmental units created lacked an operational or staff function, meaning they had little impact upon their own business units. The units were perceived by management as having no relevance to daily operational activities and therefore of low priority when allocating scarce resources to implement environmental procedures.

While it could be suggested that operational managers were guilty of staying within their knowledge comfort zone, environmental managers were also guilty of sitting back and waiting for recognition and acceptance by operational managers instead of taking the time to explain and demonstrate the benefits of an environmental policy to operational activities. They may have felt their cause was right but they failed to remember that the organization is in business to make profit for its shareholders. It is a business culture that supports profit making activities and not good causes.

The creation of such tensions was perceived as the 'green wall' (Shelton, 1994) against which some organizations' environmental strategies were stalling. The green wall grew out of persistent differences in language and culture (Haveman and Dorfman, 1999). For the most part, management recognized that their environmental management strategy was not progressing smoothly but rather than addressing the reasons why, available resources were either redirected or the initiative was abandoned completely. In short, the creation of the green wall was the result of an uneasy fit between strategic environmental management, the business functions and the inability of environmental champions to sell the environmental benefits to other corporate managers.

Some of the symptoms of hitting the green wall are identified by Shelton (1994):

* corporate downsizing;
* tight financial controls;

- competing management strategies;
- poor communications;
- clash of business cultures;
- poor planning of environmental initiatives;
- unrealistic environmental objectives leading to loss of credibility.

All of these factors, to a greater or lesser extent, act against the successful implementation of an environmental strategy. Shelton (1994), concludes that an organization's environmental management strategy has to follow one of two paths: either a path towards an interactive and integrated environmental management strategy or a path towards the green wall. These are illustrated in Figure 4.1.

Business integration depends on building a stronger understanding of the relationships between business and environmental objectives (Haveman and Dorfman, 1999). An environmental management strategy that fits with the existing business strategy, uses business language instead of technical environmental language, and is an integral part of daily operational activities would be accepted by the organization. A stand-alone environmental unit, using environmental language, operating within a matrix organization would inevitably come up against the green wall and stall.

Operational transformation

Research suggests that there are actually two levels to business integration. The first level involves employee awareness and accountability on environmental issues, which is covered by ISO 14001 target setting, auditing and reporting systems. The second level involves the integration of environmental

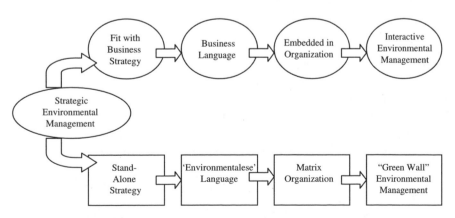

Figure 4.1   *Shelton's two paths for environmental management*

Source: Shelton (1994)

considerations into core business systems and processes (Haveman and Dorfman, 1999). ISO 14001 certification should require firms to integrate strategic environmental management into company operations through the elements of an effective EMS (Cochin, 1998). Importantly, however, the ISO 14001 standard is a process and not a performance standard so it does not mandate an organization's optimum environmental performance level but describes a system to aid the organization in achieving its own environmental objectives (Melnyk et al, 2003; Ammenberg and Sundin, 2005). This gives organizations the options to decide to what level they wish to pursue environmental performance, giving them the flexibility to develop at their own pace. However, it also means that when environmental certification is obtained, there is no guarantee that deeper operational transformation has occurred or that a cultural change, towards an ecological position, has been achieved (Ramus, 2002). Companies often have a narrow perception or knowledge of their own environmental impact, which can often limit the EMS to site-specific activities. Operational practices, those operations that the business is based on, are key to environmental transformation (Ammenberg and Sundin, 2005). Examples of operational practices are given by González-Benito and González-Benito (2005):

- Emission filters and end-of-pipe controls.
- Process and production design (design for environment), planning and control for reduced energy and natural resources consumption.
- Acquisition of clean technology.
- Preference for green products in purchasing.
- Environmental criteria in supplier selection.
- Shipment consolidation and cleaner transportation methods.
- Recyclable or reusable packaging.
- Recuperation and recycling systems.
- Responsible disposal of waste and residues.

Focusing on operational transformation requires changes in all production and management within the business to enhance a company's environmental performance. Experience from Austria, The Netherlands, Sweden and the UK shows that manufacturing environmentally friendly products or services can reduce manufacturing costs (Hui et al, 2001). However, these changes may not be perceived by customers or regulators and cannot therefore be based on commercial interests (González-Benito and González-Benito, 2005).

Design for the environment

Design for the environment (DFE) is a design competency that is currently emerging and a key to sustainable innovation and operational transformation. DFE is the adding of environmental attributes or quality factors to both products and services throughout its life cycle. Examples of ways in which DFE has been used include facilitating automation and eliminating packaging, and biodegradable or easily removed labelling to enable easier recycling of existing products (Eagan and Streckewald, 1997).

Product-oriented environmental management systems

While an EMS is a process by which many companies may first be introduced to the need for environmentally transforming operational processes and DFE, researchers have taken the EMS further to ensure that product design and development is fully integrated into the EMS. A product-oriented environmental management (POEM) system is an EMS with particular focus on the continued improvement of a product, through the systematic integration of eco-design into the company's strategies. POEM started from a policy introduced by the Dutch government with the intention of changing the behaviour of producers. A POEM system may be based on an existing EMS but adds a much stronger emphasis on life-cycle analysis and product design. A POEM system's effectiveness, along with its integration with an EMS, is not yet fully understood and requires further study. The barrier to implementing a POEM system is often the limited availability of life-cycle data or the lack of knowledge within a company to use life-cycle data. However, it is clear so far that POEM systems may be used to complement existing EMS to aid a better understanding of material flow analysis and therefore promote greater operational transformation. The POEM system models are generally based on the same Deming PDCA (Plan-Do-Check-Act) management cycle as EMSs (Ammenberg and Sundin, 2005). The main stages of a POEM system model are outlined in Table 4.3.

Hutchinson (1996) presents a checklist of criteria that demonstrates the integration of environmental policy with business strategy:

• A statement from the company's board showing commitment to integrating environmental management with business strategy and explaining the measures required to achieve this.
• Priority is given to the health and safety of employees, customers and the wider community, rather than to profit.
• The design of products, processes and services is influenced by environmental policy in an explicit way.
• Green and socially responsible purchasing is sought to avoid using scarce resources, harming endangered species or supporting oppressive regimes.
• Waste recovery is through an operating policy of minimizing waste or reuse and recycling of unavoidable waste, with a long-term aim to produce zero waste.
• Pollution is reduced at source and emissions are monitored with improvement targets set to reduce all pollution.

Table 4.3   *Main steps in a POEM system model*

Stage	Name	Key Outcomes
1	Product-specific environmental review	• Identify key aspects and impacts Review of DFE capabilities • Review of product development • Market investigation
2	Responsibilities and procedures	• Definition of roles, responsibilities and authorities for product development • Establishment of policies, objectives and targets • Revision of product development processes • Establishment of procedures for staff involved in product development and other product related activities
3	DFE projects	• Development of environmentally compatible products with competitive price, performance and quality standards
4	Audit/evaluation	• Revision of existing procedures and products aiming for continual improvement

Source: Ammenberg and Sundin (2005)

- The use of toxic substances is reduced and special care given to the handling and disposal of toxic substances that cannot be avoided.
- Packaging and products (where appropriate) are recovered, reused and recycled.
- Environmental savings are made integral to business accounting and budgeting procedures.
- Environmental training is provided when appropriate with manager rewards for environmental improvements integrated into the company's existing appraisal system.
- Continued environmental performance is considered equal to continued business improvement.
- Costs for environmental damage are included in the company's existing financial reports.

In 1999 Haveman and Dorfman studied the integration of business and environment in the company SC Johnson and devised a list of just three themes that summarize the features listed by Hutchinson (1996):

1   Redefining environmental management issues as materials-use issues – companies learn to see releases and other environmental management issues as materials-use issues.

2   Aligning environmental issues with key business goals – companies rethinking and redesigning business goals to accommodate environmental goals.
3   Designing consistency into the management system – a key issue to ensure that environmental improvement is compatible with other management goals. The management system should not send conflicting messages; it should reconcile economic and environmental objectives.

Haveman and Dorfman (1999) also acknowledge, however, that by integrating environmental issues into the core business, environmental trade-offs are required because not all environmental benefits can be achieved without economic costs. Examples of such trade-offs are:

- Reductions in packaging lead to less protection and can increase opportunities for shoplifting the product.
- Environmental modifications slow down manufacturing.
- Environmental modifications require additional training of staff.
- Environmentally beneficial materials increase the cost of production.
- Environmental modifications limit the ways in which equipment can be used.

TOWARDS A CONCEPTUAL RESEARCH MODEL

The cross-disciplinary, cross-functional nature of environmental problems creates a drive for organizational reform and revised management thinking (Roome, 1994). According to Peters and Waterman (1989), establishing individual and shared responsibility for corporate environmentalism should be replaced by more flexible organizations and a matrix of formal and informal networks. An environmental policy being introduced into an organization with a strong formalized planning process will have to overcome the inertia of an organization moving from one set of structures, systems and values to another (Quinn, 1980; Mintzberg, 1987).

Any structural change within organizations requires some organizational adaptation (Mintzberg, 1987; Ansoff, 1991). Traditional management thinking prefers incremental change when introducing change into an organization (Quinn, 1978). Senior management consensus is that incremental change, if done properly, can overcome resistance. In some companies, however, incremental change can be too slow to overcome a particular problem (Quinn, 1980). This would tend to support Shelton's (1994) theory of how management systems can stall or fail altogether.

Prior to any environmental considerations most organizations establish a formal strategy and structure for internalizing and meeting regulatory and organizational goals. The existing strategy and structures have been formed over a

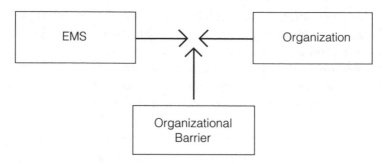

Figure 4.2   *A preliminary conceptual research model*

number of years by the organizational culture and history (Schein, 1987). The introduction of new environmental management systems challenges the traditionally conservative culture of most organizations (Smith, 1990). This turbulence pressures 'organizations to redefine their goals, to modify organizational boundaries and structures, to implant new value systems and to recognize, and support, specific types of management competence' (Roome, 1994).

Mintzberg (1987) defines strategy as being 'both a plan for the future and a pattern from the past'. He explains that intended behaviour for an organization is based on past patterns of previous action. While he admits that strategy may not have a pattern initially, and new patterns may emerge from that intended by the strategy, he contends that strategy is a craft that requires 'thought and action, control and learning, stability and change'. The goal of managers, in the first instance, when introducing new strategies, is to manage stability not change (Mintzberg, 1987). He adds that when stability is achieved the manager's job is to know when and how to introduce change.

The suggestion that an organization's past provides important clues for management that are critical for the organization's future success is supported by Greiner (1972). However, while Mintzberg (1987) advocates that management can and should maintain stability while gradually introducing change, Greiner (1972) puts forward the theory that evolution and revolution are the main determinants of strategic change. Greiner adds that these are brought about as an organization develops through size of organization, type of market and rate of organizational growth.

To synthesize the strategic theories of Mintzberg (1987) and Greiner (1972), Quinn (1978) introduces 'logical incrementalism' to aid the emergence of a strategy. He argues that it is impossible to predict all the forces and events that will shape the future of an organization. Quinn adds that the best strategies are built on a sound resource base and company posture that provides rigidity, from which to:

> *proceed incrementally to handle urgent matters, start longer term*
> *sequences whose specific future branches and consequences are perhaps*
> *murky, respond to unforeseen events as they occur, build on successes,*

and brace up or cut losses on failures. They constantly reassess the future, find new congruencies as events unfurl, and blend the organisation's skills and resources into new balances of dominance and risk aversion as various forces intersect to suggest better – but never perfect – alignments. The process is dynamic, with neither a real beginning nor end. (Quinn, 1978)

The problem with Mintzberg's (1987) theory, according to Boeker (1997), is that as the top management structure becomes more stable, senior management are less likely to deviate from the current course of action, particularly if the company is enjoying good performance. The literature (Reed and Buckley, 1988; Gallarotti, 1995; Tsai and Child, 1997) largely delineates strategy implementation as a series of individual components that need to be considered when introducing organizational strategies. These individual components include strategy–structure fit, resource allocation, executive style, organizational theory, management information systems and budgetary control.

There is little evidence, however, as to how these components react in environmental strategy implementation, or whether one component plays a more significant role at a particular phase of implementation. Patel and Younger's (1978) study explores the differences between the concept of corporate strategy and business unit strategy. They found that corporate strategies are primarily focused on business unit configuration, management systems and financial transactions with a view to corporate growth and profitability. Business unit strategy, they found, is primarily concerned with competitive advantage.

5

Linking Environmental Management with Business Strategy

INTRODUCTION

As guides to the effectiveness of environmental management systems and their development within an organization environmental models and performance indicators can be argued to be useful. However, it can also be argued that they are two dimensional, failing to explore the competitive advantage of integrating an EMS with the existing business strategy. This chapter explores six case studies that facilitate the development of four new models that link environmental management with business strategy to offer new competitive advantage opportunities.

BACKGROUND

For each type of model discussed in Chapter 4, four key characteristics can be identified:

- organizational profile;
- operational advantages;
- operational disadvantages;
- organizational barriers.

By assessing these characteristics, four categorical models can be constructed to demonstrate the typical profile of organizations. These models categorize those organizations that are 'devoid' of an EMS or have one that is 'isolated', 'devolved' or 'integrated' within the organization (Tinsley, 2002). Case studies of each of these categories are given below. Each includes a table that explores the overall theoretical characteristics of each type, followed by the case study and a table of the particular characteristics of the company. Comparisons of the theoretical characteristics and the case studies show that the unique circumstances of a company never fit exactly into theory. However, it is also illustrated that the classifications of devoid, isolated, devolved and integrated EMSs can be useful on a broad scale to help understand the consequences of different approaches.

DEVOID EMS MODEL

The devoid EMS model is illustrated in Table 5.1 and includes organizations that may have an EMS but have not had it accredited. Also included are those organizations that are currently in the process of implementing an accredited EMS. Those in the process of implementation should have a lower environmental risk and reduced operational disadvantages, however, work by Shelton (1994) shows that there is risk within organizations that are in the process of implementing EMSs but that have either stalled or failed to complete an EMS to full accreditation. Certification is a confirmation by a third party that a company is successfully addressing their environmental issues. Lack of certification can mean that the EMS is not being monitored and verified, giving a company no security that it is working sufficiently to ensure even basic compliance (Morrow and Rondinelli, 2002). In the worst case scenario, all the resources and effort that

Table 5.1 *Devoid EMS model*

EMS Model	Devoid
Organizational Profile	No accredited EMS
	In the process of installing an accredited EMS
Operational Advantages	None
Operational Disadvantages	High risk of heavy fines
	Adverse publicity
	Lack of shareholder investment
	Loss of credibility
	High investment risk
	Loss of competitive advantage
	Loss of market share
	Not accepted on many major supply chains
	High risk of environmental incident
Organizational Barriers	Management commitment
	Communication
	Available resources
	Management style
	Incentives and controls
	Credible plans
	Company culture

have gone into implementing an EMS may be considered wasted if it cannot ensure compliance.

Organizations can operate waste monitoring and energy efficiency schemes without requiring an accredited EMS, thereby accruing some benefits. However, a number of operational disadvantages result from not having an accredited EMS and these add up to a high-risk strategy. Many of those organizational barriers identified in the literature and discussed in Chapter 3 are likely to occur in an organization devoid of an EMS.

An organization within the devoid EMS model is found to delay or abandon the pursuit of an EMS during an economic downturn. Scarce resources are redirected to operational activities and the implementation of an accredited EMS is left until economic conditions improve. This model carries a high risk of an environmental incident occurring.

Some managers may consider that an operational benefit can accrue by redirecting scarce resources to operational, as opposed to, non-operational activities. Due to the number of pieces of environmental legislation and regulation currently in force (Ball and Bell, 1997) and the lack of operational efficiency resulting from not having an accredited EMS, it is considered that there are no operational advantages to be gained from using this model.

Case study of devoid EMS: Company A

Background
Company A is a camera manufacturing company with facilities based in Scotland that employs approximately 1000 employees and is made up of five manufacturing divisions:

1 hardware division;
2 film manufacture;
3 pocket film;
4 design and development;
5 sunglass lenses.

The hardware division comprises the integral camera assembly process. Parts and sub-assemblies are bought in from around the world and assembled either on production lines or in small production modules. Significant proportions of the shutter sub-assemblies are manufactured on a robotic line. This division produces over a million cameras every year. The film manufacture division is largely a customized integrated flow process, at the heart of which is the film pack assembly process. In the design and build assembly unit, the major photographic components are brought together to form the film pack. Another customized integrated flow process is at the heart of the pocket film division. Here sub-assemblies are laminated together to form a strip that is then inserted into a small black box to make up the pack of film. Output here exceeds 4 million packs per annum. Over the past few years the site has become the design and development centre for new products. These products are exported all over the world. The fifth division manufactures polarized plastic lenses from laminate sheet. The sheet is cut and formed into finished optical lenses.

Interview with Company A

Company A began implementing its EMS, ISO 14001, in the hope of gaining final certification in just over one year. Their two main drivers for implementing ISO 14001 are first, to follow good practice and second, to continually improve business operations.

The environmental manager who was interviewed had been with the company for 22 years and had been involved with environmental projects for 11 years. He reports to the UK health, safety and environment manager. They are the two main people responsible for the implementation of the EMS.

Top management commitment

The commitment of top management to the EMS is minimal; the environmental manager commented that 'they are committed to seeing the system implemented with the minimum use of manufacturing resources'. Company A directors and managers do not consider that their company's activities pose any serious environmental threat. They all believe that an EMS is required for manufacturing activities only. The EMS is therefore supported but only on a minimum cost basis. There is sufficient legislative pressure in the UK and Europe for Company A to make a policy decision for all manufacturing plants in the UK and Europe to achieve ISO 14001. This is not a requirement in the US as environmental legislative pressures are minimal. Company A's plants in the US will follow suit when environmental pressures increase to those of Europe and the UK.

Organizational structure

The existing organizational structure is considered by management not to have an impact on system implementation because the EMS only affects the manufacturing departments. In fact, to many managers and directors, the implementation of the EMS is seen as a hindrance. It is seen as consuming valuable manufacturing resources for non-operational activities. The environmental manager felt that 'it was this attitude that has already delayed the implementation of the EMS by six months'.

System integration

Company A views the implementation of ISO 14001 as a 'stand-alone' system. Company A does not intended to integrate the EMS with the other management systems, such as health and safety, which is also treated as a stand-alone system. The lack of commitment from staff to the EMS is as a direct result of a lack of integration of the EMS. Senior managers are also sending the wrong signals to employees; at present there are two manufacturing staff who are tasked with the responsibility of implementing ISO 14001, but the environmental manager felt that 'these people are given the task of implementation until other operational commitments call them away, they are then replaced with two different staff members. Consequently, implementation continuity is adversely affected'.

Managers and directors believe that the existing quality and health and safety system will take care of any environmental legislative requirements. Impending Waste Electrical and Electronic Equipment and Packaging directives will be documented as part of the EMS, which will be integrated with the existing quality system.

The controls for the monitoring and running of the EMS remain as per the existing management reporting system. The quality manager reporting on quality issues will also be responsible for reporting on environmental and health and safety issues. The two main areas of the quality manager's reporting focus will be first, the reporting of best practice in the manufacturing process and second, reporting on environmental issues or pressures. Best practice is thus a Company A objective and considerable attention will be given to manufacturing best practice and to the environmental requirements to ensure it.

In the US, due to the lack of environmental legislation requiring environmental management change, the company is considered to be environmentally low risk. There is currently no pressure from US to develop an EMS standard. The implementation of the ISO 14001 system is purely to improve manufacturing efficiency, that is less waste, less energy usage, improved design and manufacturing processes. As a consequence the EMS is considered by the environmental manager to be 'invisible to a lot of people and not applicable to the whole company'.

Available resources

Resources are limited for the implementation of the EMS. Senior managers had agreed that a budget was available but its size was never specified. Separate cases were made to senior management for the level and timing of expenditure. According to the environmental manager: 'Sometimes cases were approved and sometimes not. The two managers tasked with the implementation of the system also had full-time, often conflicting, operational jobs. This is not a workable arrangement.'

To assist with the increased workload, a dedicated person was to be seconded to the manufacturing department for six months to write procedures and work instructions. After three months, nobody has yet been identified to fill the position, the reason being that they could not find anyone who was suitably qualified. Suggestions have been put forward by the two incumbent managers to use a post-graduate student of EMS at the dissertation stage in exchange for some work experience.

Innovation

There are three main business goals for Company A's Scottish site: first, to grow the company; second, to regenerate existing products; and third, to appeal to a younger market. The EMS would become a subset of the first business objective as the emphasis is to grow the company on environmentally sound products. The growth objective will also include developing and adopting innovative ideas in plant technology to make processes more efficient and less harmful to the environment; 'there is certainly considerable management commitment to adopting new technology,' said the environmental manager.

Communication

Communication of the company objectives is considered to be very good. The company intranet is used to provide information on many aspects of company activity including environmental and quality issues. The intranet is plant-wide and delivers the outcomes of quarterly business meetings and quarterly newsletters, including those items that promote environmental development to all employee levels. Spreadsheets are posted showing the progress of many waste collection and energy saving schemes.

Credible plans

The plans for the introduction of the EMS are considered credible in as much as they 'affect a minimum amount of people and there are minor high-risk activities'. Incentives for their achievement are considered adequate. The environmental manager's view is that: 'we do not get a lot of hassle from third parties seeking environmental information, the implementation of the EMS is driven by the manufacturing unit and there is no demand or pressure from other areas of the organization or from the general public.'

Follow-up interview

Company A was originally interviewed, and their EMS assessed, when there were strong economic conditions in their sector. An opportunity arose to interview the organization following a downturn in this industry sector. It was felt that a follow-up interview would provide insight into whether their EMS model remained consistent in negative economic conditions.

The interview was undertaken by telephone with the same environmental manager. It was unstructured with the interviewee asked to recall the original interview conversation and to compare the situation then and to comment on the aspects of the economic downturn. The participant was asked to relate the economic changes that the organization was currently experiencing and to identify any factors that were having an effect on the EMS.

Company A had announced that 235 of their 1750 employees were to be made redundant, considered by Company A to be a 'drastic cutback'. A key directive from senior management had asked managers to 'do what you can but spend no money'. Another senior management directive stated that the implementation of the EMS would be shelved for one year. There was no budget allocation for EMS implementation.

Company A's senior management team still held to the notion that their organization was not a high environmental risk. There was no pressure from customers and the message from their corporate office in the US was that there was no environmental management pressure as long as the EMS was not ignored completely. The waste recycling programmes that had previously been set up remained in place and a system audit would be completed. The plan, identified in the first interview, to employ a post-graduate student to write the ISO 14001 procedures has also been delayed for one year. The new target for achieving ISO 14001 certification, is now two years later than first anticipated.

The key directive from the US is that Company A's existing product range has achieved market maturity and that the priority for all available resources is the development of new products. This, together with the loss and movement of people, has resulted in a decline in commitment by departments to the EMS. It is anticipated that when the implementation of the EMS is activated again next year, there will have to be a new environmental awareness and training programme undertaken.

Devoid EMS profile

By selecting the key characteristics of the Company A case study, the following profile (Table 5.2) is that of an organization that is devoid of an environmental management system.

Isolated EMS model

The characteristics of an organization with an isolated EMS model are shown in table 5.3. An organization with an isolated EMS profile will have an accredited system. This may only apply to one part of the organization (manufacturing) or to the whole organization, with a small team established in an isolated unit to deal with environmental compliance issues.

An isolated EMS, by its very nature, is separated from many of the daily operations of the organization. As a consequence there is a lack of communication of the environmental team trying to raise levels of awareness and have input into operational decisions with other managers. Limited resources were used to establish the unit and this sends the message to employees and managers that there is a lack of commitment from senior managers and directors and that environmental issues have low priority against operational requirements.

Table 5.2   *Devoid profile of Company A*

Characteristics of Company A: Devoid EMS	No accredited EMS
Organizational Drivers	Improve efficiency
	Minimize environmental risk
	To remain competitive
Operational Advantages	Communications is believed to be good
Operational Disadvantages	High risk of heavy fines
	Adverse publicity
	Lack of shareholder investment
	Loss of credibility
	High investment risk
	Loss of competitive advantage
	Loss of market share
	Not accepted on many major supply chains
	High risk of environmental incident
Organizational Barriers	Management commitment limited
	Organizational structure considered to be irrelevant
	System integration limited.
	Available resources very limited including trained staff
	Innovation wanted but not investigated
	Credible plans not formulated

Case study of isolated EMS: Company B

Company B commenced business 100 years ago by entering the communications equipment market. In 1950 transistor-oriented research and development led to the beginning of Company B's semiconductor business. They entered the computer market in 1954 with the start of an extensive computer-related research and development programme. They have achieved their growth today through the formation of strategic alliances with other successful companies to provide a range of high technology products and services.

The organization's main products and services include the provision of internet business solutions and the manufacture and sales of computers, communications equipment, electronic devices and software.

Table 5.3   *Isolated EMS model*

EMS Model	Isolated
Organizational Profile	The organization has an accredited EMS
	The EMS applies to only a part of the organization
	A small unit or team has been established to deal with environmental compliance
Operational Advantages	Low cost option focused only on compliance
Operational Disadvantages	Low priority of environmental issues
	Loss of efficiency
	Fire-fighting environmental incidents
Organizational Barriers	Communication
	Management commitment
	Available resources
	Incentives and controls
	Company culture
	Credible plans
	Management style
	Organizational structure

Company B has a plant in Scotland that was established in 1981 and after three development phases has a facility of 500,000 square metres and employs approximately 1500 people in semiconductor manufacturing.

Interview
The environmental manager was interviewed for this case study. He has been with the company for 16 years and involved with the EMS for four years. ISO 14001 is the EMS being used and certification was achieved three years ago. He was involved with the ISO 14001 system during implementation and certification. He reports directly to the general manager of Company B.

Incentives and organizational strategy
The two main drivers for the introduction of the EMS were first, responding to customer and public demands and second, a directive from corporate office requesting that all plants worldwide were to be certified to ISO 14001. The corporate office has assumed responsibility for the administration and auditing of the EMS at all sites.

Culture and management commitment

The corporate culture is considered conducive to a strong commitment to environmental, health and safety, and quality issues. The minimization of environmental risk is one of the main corporate objectives and all levels of management agree and support these main objectives. The three management systems of environment, health and safety, and quality are important to the daily manufacturing process. Managers are committed to small activity groups, similar to 'quality circles' to ensure that the standards of the three systems are maintained.

Controls

While head office takes a broad product-based approach, device manufacturing varies from site to site and it is the responsibility of each site to be more focused on the detail of the environmental issues that emerge and the different types of devices and manufacturing processes used.

Integrated systems

At present there are three separate management systems: environment, health and safety, and quality. Discussions are ongoing as to the benefits of an integrated environment and health and safety management system. The current preference is to merge the two and keep quality as a separate system. The reasoning is that the quality system is so intensive and technical because of the nature of semiconductor manufacture that it should not be diluted. Over time the expectancy is that the three systems will eventually merge as one system due to the ongoing merging of ISO standard requirements.

Strategy complexity

The three systems currently operate separately leading to some complexity. This is not considered to be too disruptive as long as each system is part of daily operational activity and that the administration of the three systems is similar. The environmental manager admitted that 'the technical complexity will remain with the quality system but this is the nature of our business. There is often crossover of system operations but the environmental function is clearly understood by everyone.'

Communication

To ensure clear understanding, communication is deemed important and there are a number of training programmes and briefing meetings that managers and staff can feed into. There are adequate resources for the development of existing and new communication projects. Although identified as being important for environmental communication and awareness programmes, information technology is little used at present. Environmental documents and procedures are kept in electronic format although not everyone has access to them. An environmental website is currently being developed but is not yet in operation.

Incentives

The environmental manager believes that despite the lack of financial incentives, existing employee recognition programmes provide sufficient incentives for employees and managers to achieve targets. The company newsletter provides one outlet where people can be recognized for achieving environmental targets or identifying innovative ideas. On the subject of innovation he suggested that: 'many of the innovative ideas that have emerged to benefit the organization have done so as a consequence of having an EMS, without it I'm sure many would not have emerged; the EMS is a driver for innovation.'

Control

The environmental manager believes that because he reports directly to the managing director, resources are more easily accessed. Environmental planning also has greater credibility as environmental and operational requirements have a project focus. Resources are allocated to meet all of the projects' requirements and environmental issues are included in this. Control is strong with the environmental plans being reviewed every six months as part of the main auditing structure. At present individual sites do their own auditing; this is done on a monthly basis and the managing director is a regular participant. He is kept fully informed and if additional resources are required he is well placed to aid further commitment.

Operational transformation

When asked to identify two factors that would improve or impede the existing EMS, the environmental manager felt that significant improvement has been made since the EMS has become integrated with daily operational activities. He felt that this has helped the organization to be more transparent when environmental information has been requested by customers and the general public.

Communication

A lack of environmental awareness and the selling of the EMS's benefits, particularly to managers, impedes the development of the EMS. According to the interviewee:

> in the early days of EMS implementation this was considered important and during the implementation process it was a benefit, but what seems to have been forgotten is that these issues are still important particularly as personnel, departments and corporate objectives and targets change.

Resources

Like all companies, Company B has faced business difficulties. To date it has not announced any redundancies but they are watching the electronics industry closely. Four people make up the EMS team and they are still in position. The environmental manager suggested that:

> *while there is a restriction on expenditure, there is a reluctance to interfere with the EMS because it is fundamental to the whole manufacturing process. If the economic conditions persist the rate of continual improvement may slow but the integrity of the systems would remain.*

Isolated EMS profile

An isolated EMS (Table 5.4) is separated from other quality and health and safety systems. Individual project groups are 'quality circles' responsible for environmental considerations. There is a direct reporting line to managing director.

Table 5.4   *Isolated profile of Company B*

Characteristics of Company B: Isolated EMS	The organization has an accredited EMS
Organizational Drivers	Minimize environmental risk
	Market and customer pressures
Operational Advantages	Greater environmental openness with customers and regulatory bodies
	New project development include potential environmental impact assessment
Operational Disadvantages	Lack of environmental awareness
	Degree of environmental prioritizing behind operational needs
	Environmental resources dependent upon project approval
Organizational Barriers	Administrative complexity of three independent systems
	Lack of adequate IT structure
	Available resources determined on a project-to-project basis
	Lack of management commitment

DEVOLVED EMS MODEL

An organization operating with a devolved EMS has an accredited system that pervades the whole organization and is part of daily operational activities. It is likely that the manager responsible for environmental management will also be responsible for health and safety, and possibly quality. The responsible manager will play a key administrative role by communicating progress to senior management by way of periodic reports and ensuring that training and awareness programmes are made available for employee use. Contractors responsible for specific tasks of waste recycling and energy efficiency monitoring will report to the organization's environmental manager.

The key operational advantage that a devolved system offers is one of flexibility. The use of contract staff can aid this flexibility by hiring or downsizing whenever the economic situation dictates. The high hourly rates of engagement are considered an acceptable price to pay for this flexibility. While the organization administers the system, there is a danger downsizing operations will cause the loss of environmental knowledge and experience of operational processes.

This style of management is seen as a key organizational barrier to the development of an EMS as the focus is on short-term costs and not on long-term environmental improvement. Communication is also considered a barrier as contractors constantly change and communications can be interrupted. A 'them and us' attitude between organizational staff and contractors can lead to informal demarcation lines and grey areas of responsibility.

Case study of devolved model: Company C

Background
In 1999 Company C split from its parent company and was listed as a public company on the New York Stock Exchange. Company C operates four

Table 5.5 *Devolved EMS model*

EMS Model	Devolved EMS
Organizational Profile	The organization has an accredited EMS Key manager provides an administration support function for contractor activities
Operational Advantages	Increased downsizing flexibility
Operational Disadvantages	High cost option
	Loss of environmental knowledge and expertise
Organizational Barriers	Gaps in communication
	Management style

businesses: test and measurement, semiconductor products, healthcare solutions and chemical analysis, supported by a central laboratory. Its businesses apply measurement technologies to develop products that sense, analyse, display and communicate data. Company C's customers include many of the world's leading high-technology firms, which rely on Company C's products and services to make them more profitable and competitive, from research and development through to manufacturing, installation and maintenance. Company C enables its customers to speed their time to market and to achieve volume production and high quality, precision manufacturing.

A key driver for Company C's products and services is the pervasive transformation from analogue to digital technology. Because digital technologies require greater degrees of precision and rely more on miniature circuitry, the role of test and measurement is 'mission critical' for the rapid commercialization of reliable internet-age products.

Company C has 48,000 employees and facilities in more than 40 countries serving market leading customers in over 120 countries. Major product development and manufacturing sites are located in the US, China, Germany, Japan, Malaysia, Singapore, Australia and the UK. More than half of the company's net revenue is derived from outside the US.

The Company C site based in Scotland operates in the telecommunications testing industry sector providing industrial test equipment to major telecommunication product manufacturers. It employs 1200 people in a manufacturing site of approximately 300,000 square metres. The site separated from its parent company in 2000 having originally been the testing facility for the parent company.

Interview

The person interviewed was the product steward manager who is responsible for ensuring that a high percentage of recyclable material is designed into Company C's products. He has been with the organization for three years and is involved with ISO 14001 environmental management system. He reports to the manufacturing engineering manager.

He sees the two main drivers for the organization having an EMS as first, to remain competitive and second, to reduce environmental risk. These drivers were initially part of the parent company's corporate policy. Company C was originally the 'beta' test site for the introduction of ISO 14001. After the separation, the EMS remained with the new business because the operations remained the same.

Management commitment and management style

Despite the separation, senior management remained committed to the EMS and applied a corporate directive to other sites to introduce ISO 14001. At present the commitment from senior management to reduce environmental risk is considered strong. The organizational structure is flatter than that of the parent company and more devolved. When the company still belonged to its parent, it was more difficult to get senior management to support environmental management issues due to the increased number of organizational layers. A consequence of this structure was that there were more political considerations and there were more business/environment trade-offs.

The product steward manager believes that within Company C the management style is less autocratic than the parent company and seems more suited to cope with a higher level of environmental risk. However, environmental management is never a high priority because of the nature of the business. He pointed to the fact that:

> *because we produce low volume, high quality industrial products and not commercial products, we have no consumer pressure groups driving environmental standards. We do, however, listen to our major product purchasing clients who expect us to adhere to their environmental standards, but here there is not the same pressure. The existing corporate culture does aid the development of the EMS, but due to the current economic circumstances it is not top priority. It is still very much part of our daily operational process and product design but just as with quality and health and safety the speed of development may slow.*

Prior to the industry downturn, senior management was more committed to addressing the development of the EMS. The product steward manager accepts that the main reason for this would have been as a result of the split from the parent company. He added that:

> *much environmental expertise had been lost through the departure of personnel and much EMS knowledge and experience was, and is still required to incorporate the products and services of Company C as opposed to the parent company's original computer manufacturing activities.*

Resources
The interviewee believes that 'the EMS development commitment still exists, not just on the Scottish site but across other sites in the UK too, but it is the current lack of available resources that will slow the development of the EMS.' Initially, with the parent company, strong economic periods signalled significant available resources. Following the split, significant resources were also made available for the revamping of the ISO 14001 standard to Company C's products. During the sector downturn resources are no longer so abundant but this applies across the

organization, not just to the EMS. According to the product steward manager: 'Having an integrated system means that if daily operational activity decreases everything that is associated with it also decreases.'

The interviewee believes that information technology plays a large part in the system integration process because the guidelines, documents and procedures for the EMS and the other systems are almost all based on a paperless system. The signing of documents and procedures is also done electronically. He commented that 'our passive approval documentation process means that the document or procedure is seen by everyone and is accepted unless an objection is raised. This speeds everything up, although caution does have to be exercised.'

System integration

All of the management information systems such as environment, quality and health and safety are integrated into a single system: 'This system was planned by senior management, following the split from the parent company, as a method to improve efficiency and reduce operating costs.' It was considered that as there was a database of legislation affecting the organization, it did not matter whether it was environmental or health and safety related; it was relevant to how the product was designed and manufactured. Quality is also built into the design and manufacturing of the products so it is considered that an integrated approach works.

Strategic complexity

There is little complexity as plans, procedures and controls for the EMS are based on those guidelines provided as part of the ISO 14001 and ISO 9001 standards currently being worked to. He added:

> we do not want to reinvent the wheel. Communication plays a big part in reducing complexity. Following the 'split' it was essential to ensure the company operated effectively as a separate entity. Within Company C there is currently an ongoing project to integrate all databases into one large, centralized database – at times we can suffer from having too much information.

Incentives

For the majority of employees there are no financial incentives to reward them for an EMS that operates efficiently and develops continuously. Recognition for new ideas for waste reduction or energy efficiency schemes is given in the corporate newsletter. Some senior and middle managers do have some financial incentives for environmental improvement but these would have been individually negotiated into their contracts of employment. In the current economic climate it is felt that financial incentives would be difficult to justify, particularly as all employees, managers included, have recently been asked to consider a 10 per cent salary reduction in order to avoid redundancies.

The two most difficult areas for the EMS at present are first, the lack of EMS champions within the organization that have influence among senior managers and second, the lack of short-term environmental benefits that can be traded-off with senior management for investment into long-term environmental improvements. The interviewee suggested that 'the short business cycles from product development to obsolescence and trying to sell the long-term benefits of proposed environmental product improvements, can at times, be difficult to reconcile.'

Innovation

It is recognized that there is a need for innovation within the EMS but at present, possibly because of the split, the most innovative ideas are being used to put forward arguments to obtain additional investment for long-term environmental improvements.

Current economic situation

In addition to the proposal that the workforce accept a 10 per cent reduction in pay, Company C is closely monitoring the redundancy programmes of its major clients within the electronics and telecommunications sector.

Devolved EMS profile

Contractors are responsible for carrying our environmental duties and the organizational manager has multiple tasks, a reporting administrative function to senior managers and a communications function to all employees. EMS is integrated with health and safety, and quality systems, and information technology plays an important part in EMS administration.

Case study of devolved model: Company D

Background

With more than 12 million printers sold since the company was founded in 1972, Company D is recognized as a leader among PC peripheral (printers, facsimile and multifunction products) companies in the US, Canada and Latin America.

Company D's parent company is a US$5.6 billion multinational corporation and a world leader in information processing systems, telecommunications and electronics. It is ranked first among impact printer manufacturers in North America with a 37 per cent market share, and is ranked second among vendors

Table 5.6 *Devolved profile of Company C*

Characteristics of Company C: Devolved EMS	The organization has an accredited EMS
Organizational Drivers	Minimize environmental risk
	To remain competitive
Operational Advantages	Standardized system administration – one information database
	Flexibility to expand and downsize quickly
	Innovation comes to the fore
	Operational disadvantages
	Organization has flat structure
	Managers have more hands-on role, closer to daily operations
Operational Disadvantages	High cost of operational flexibility
	Potential for loss of knowledge and experience
	Lack of EMS champions
	Lack of long-term environmental investment
Organizational Barriers	Lack of available resources
	Lack of communications
	Lack of management commitment
	Speed of organizational change

in the 1–10 ppm laser category with a 6.5 per cent market share (Dataquest, 1999).

It has one of the broadest product lines in the industry, marketed under the brand name and including printer technologies of dot matrix, digital light emitter displays and colour and monochrome. Company D's site in Scotland is the main supplier for Europe and employs 900 people on a manufacturing site of 250,000 square metres.

Interview

The person interviewed was the environmental manager. He has been with the company for 11 years and involved with the EMS throughout the implementation process that began in May 1997 and culminated with final certification in April 1998. He reports to the operations support general manager who is responsible for the manufacturing support services that include the environmental, quality and health and safety systems.

The main drivers for the organization having an EMS have changed over a number of years. In 1992 there were two main drivers: first, adhering to existing environmental legislation, and second, market pressure. In 1996 a third driver was added by way of the implementation of a corporate directive requiring all manufacturing sites to have an accredited EMS based on the ISO 14001 standard.

This corporate directive ensured commitment from senior management. Prior to 1996 senior management commitment for the EMS was sporadic and varied from site to site, hence attitudes towards environmental responsibility mirrored differences in cultural attitudes in Japan, the US and Europe. Environmental issues were considered to be low priority and not part of the corporate culture.

The plant in Scotland began with three distinct management systems: environment, quality and health and safety. The objective for the plant is to eventually have one fully integrated management system incorporating all three systems. The roles of the environment, quality and health and safety managers will eventually merge to form a team of individuals that will be responsible for site facilities management.

The role restructuring will have the effect of flattening the organizational structure and current plans are designed to continue this process, aiding the development of one fully integrated system. The environmental manager considers that this is a good move as 'managers are getting closer to the operational "front line" and are becoming more aware of the daily operational and environmental requirements.'

Integrated systems

Effective administration of an integrated system is also important. Most of the environmental documents and procedures are in electronic format but that is not sufficient according to the environmental manager, he felt that 'to enable a fully integrated system a more focused approach is required on the use of IT.'

At present the existing word documents and intranet services are considered wholly inadequate for the proposed integrated system. Software packages do exist to aid an integrated system but research is still underway to determine whether existing 'off-the-shelf' software packages are suitable or whether a customized software package needs to be written. He believes that:

> managers accept that there are many similarities between the three management systems, which is a big step forward. The use of software for an integrated management system will only work if the administration of the systems is standardized. The integration of an EMS will also require the 'cross-training' of auditors to audit all systems.

Credible plans

When asked about how credible the plans were for the move to an integrated environmental system, the environmental manager remarked:

> *Initially, for the introduction of the EMS we followed the BSI guidelines for 14001 but as we have developed the system so further plans have been presented by management. As we are not sure how to progress to a fully integrated system, these plans are being written as we speak and they will have to be approved by senior management before they are accepted. There may be a possibility that this site takes on the environmental responsibilities for a European site and we will have to amend our EMS plans again.*

The feeling among managers until just recently was that an integrated environment, health and safety, and quality system was not needed. The environmental manager felt that the three systems could exist quite successfully separately. However, he commented that 'the recent downturn in the electronics industry is leading to a rapid move to a more integrated system to aid flexibility and reduce costs.' He believes that:

> *Integration has been somewhat thrust upon us but, on the positive side, it provides an opportunity to think about the systems and consider their efficiency and effectiveness. We anticipate improvement from a long hard look at what the systems are there to do and the roles of personnel within the systems.*

Communication

The continual changes make communication an important issue within the organization. Frequent change puts pressure on the internal communications structure to keep all employees informed. This communication process will be strained further with the current economic changes as some employees will be made redundant, some will have new responsibilities and some contractors will be used as more environmental services are outsourced.

Resources

These changes will also put a strain on available resources. Initially, there were sufficient finances and people to support the operation of the environmental, quality and health and safety systems but now, as a result of the restructuring, a number of people have been lost from the EMS:

> *The energy manager and the facilities manager have been made redundant and most of their responsibilities have been given to me along*

with a, still to be confirmed, title of 'site facilities manager'. The remaining environmental personnel are mostly contract personnel.

Resources at the moment are scarce and each environmental project has to be presented and approved on its merits by senior management.

It was felt that the increased use of contractors as opposed to employees would allow the organization to be more flexible in its operations as these could be turned on and off depending on the economic circumstances. The downsides were perceived as the expense of constantly changing personnel and the loss of environmental knowledge, experience and responsibility. The constant process of change would lead to the continual reinvention of the environmental management wheel but not necessarily continuous improvement – the ethos of the ISO 14001 standard. It was considered that the greater the rate of change, the harder it is to build awareness and maintain environmental commitment. Conversely, if change is too slow, apathy can creep in. Some change is good for continual improvement but a high rate of change can create chaos.

Current changes to the organization include moving the manufacturing facility to Thailand and reducing employee numbers from 900 to 500. It is perceived that everything will have to be realigned with the reduced business requirements, including procedures and systems. The organization will have to go through the awareness cycle again as some people will have left and others have changed responsibilities. This will affect all employee levels.

Losing people from the environmental and health and safety functions has been added to the workload. According to the environmental manager:

> *This requires us to devolve some functions to external consultants, particularly auditing. People have been demoted, promoted and the whole organizational structure has been flattened. Middle management has been stripped out. Environmental budgets remain but they have been reduced along with everything else. Problems are being experienced even now with devolving responsibility and levels of professionalism.*

It is perceived that operating with a flat structure means that the main focus is on cost. The environmental principle of 'best available techniques not entailing excessive cost' (BATNEEC) is used to assess the viability of every environmental project:

> *We are now working with financial targets as opposed to environmental targets. Environmental priorities are low priority by necessity. We work within economic constraints where the emphasis is on balance. Budgets for all systems are required to go further.*

With the loss of key personnel the management of three separate systems would be a complex mix, thus it is hoped that the streamlining of the three systems into one will alleviate the complexity. The interviewee felt he was being forced to consider what the organization is trying to achieve and therefore cut out the dead wood:

> *Innovation is beginning to come to the fore, working on the assumption that 'necessity is the mother of invention', the lack of resources is forcing us to consider innovative ways of overcoming environmental issues. One recent example was the reduction of the high cost of disposing of condensate trade effluent; a new separation system was designed and built to separate oil and waste and divert to soakaways. This averted an expensive draining system that was originally planned to cope with the produced condensate.*

Innovation

It is thought that innovation could play a bigger part in the EMS development process for Company D if there was a greater emphasis on incentives and rewards for new ideas. At present there are no financial incentives for environmental ideas development, the site newsletter provides the only forum through which to acknowledge the efforts of staff. Some incentive is provided at the induction process where employees and contractors are advised of waste recycling and energy efficiency schemes. Monthly management meetings also exist to give managers the opportunity to encourage existing employees in the pursuit of environmental targets.

It is perceived that there is a real danger that the continual changes to numbers and responsibilities of employees will lead environmental issues to be forgotten about. As well as the strong emphasis on the induction process, individual employee appraisal programmes act as a sufficient control system to ensure that a high level of environmental awareness is maintained. Regular environmental management reviews are also considered to be of assistance. It is hoped that, given current economic conditions, the frequency of these two important control mechanisms will remain and not be reduced.

It is not considered that the EMS is being reduced in itself because environmental issues are part of the daily activities of the company and the overall operational budget allocation. Instead, it is being downsized together with other management systems and operational requirements. The environmental manager argued that: 'the organization is striving for balance not excellence, after all we are in competition with our own sites as well as those of our competitors.'

Current economic situation

Company D has announced that they will reduce their workforce from 900 to 500 over the next six months. Their manufacturing facility will be closed down and transferred to one of their plants in Thailand. The Scottish site will act purely as a packaging and distribution centre for products from the rest of the world that are destined for Europe.

Devolved EMS profile

As with Company C, contractors are responsible for carrying out environmental duties and the organizational manager has multiple tasks, a reporting and administrative function to senior mangers and a communications function to all employees. Integrating EMS with health and safety, quality systems and IT plays an important part in EMS administration.

INTEGRATED EMS MODEL

An organization with an integrated EMS incorporates their environmental, health and safety (H&S) and quality systems into one system. The single systems are often renamed as an environmental health and safety (EHS) systems and are designed to operate with the same documents and procedures and 'cross-skilled' auditors to monitor the system.

The key operational benefit of an integrated EMS is that it becomes part of daily operational activities. It is a system that is part of the organization's goals and objectives and as such it has the commitment of all managers and directors.

Table 5.7   *Devolved profile of Company D*

Characteristics of Company D: Devolved EMS	The organization has an accredited EMS
Organizational Drivers	Minimize environmental risk
	Market and customer pressure for environmentally sound products and services
Operational Advantages	Organization has flat structure, managers have more hands on role and are closer to daily operations
	Flexibility to expand and downsize quickly
	Innovation comes to the fore
	Standardized system administration
Operational Disadvantages	High cost of operational flexibility
	Loss of knowledge and experience
	Less environmental control
Organizational Barriers	Lack of available resources
	Lack of communications
	Lack of management commitment
	Speed of organizational change

Monitoring daily operational activities gives management early warning of the development of potential environmental incidents. The development of an integrated EMS will give the organization an opportunity to develop a culture of continuous improvement.

An operational disadvantage that can occur is that the establishment of a corporate centralized auditing unit can result in loss of intimate environmental knowledge of site-specific manufacturing processes. Additionally, an audit programme may structure the required audits to be undertaken every two or three months, but some site-specific processes may require more regular audits and as such the early identification of potential environmental incidents may go undetected until they fully develop.

There seem to be few key organizational barriers that can occur with an integrated EMS, however, communication is still important to maintain employee awareness and participation. Many environmental training and awareness programmes exist within the organization but difficulties can result from a lack of employee participation. The daily interaction of environmental issues with operational activities may render them uninteresting over time. Communication is the key to keeping the environmental training and awareness programmes fresh in employees' minds. This may involve periodically changing the scope of the programmes or introducing competitions and offering cash prizes or holidays.

Although managers and directors all agree to support an EMS, there is an element of interpretation. There can be many management styles within an organization and these different styles may interpret environmental management in different ways. The outcome may be disagreement on the operational methods to be used to achieve the environmental objectives.

Table 5.8   *Integrated EMS model*

EMS Model	Integrated EMS
Organizational Profile	The organization has an accredited EMS
	EMS is customized to fit with H&S and quality systems to form one system (e.g. EHS)
Operational Advantages	Part of daily operational activities
	Early warning of potential incidents
	Culture of continuous improvement
Operational Disadvantages	Centralized auditing process can lead to loss of site process knowledge
Organizational Barriers	Lack of employee participation
	Communication
	Management style

Case study of integrated model: Company E

Background

The company's first product was a 'battery eliminator' allowing consumers to operate radios directly from household current instead of the batteries supplied with early models. In the 1930s the organization successfully commercialized car radios. During this period, it also established home radio and police radio departments, instituted pioneering personnel programmes and began national advertising.

The decade of the 1940s also saw the organization begin government work and open a research laboratory in Phoenix, Arizona, to explore solid-state electronics. By the 1960s, Company E was a leader in military, space and commercial communications, had built its first semiconductor facility and was a growing manufacturer of consumer electronics.

Company E expanded into international markets in the 1960s and began shifting its focus away from consumer electronics. The colour television receiver business was sold in the mid-1970s, allowing Company E to concentrate its energies on high-technology markets in commercial, industrial and government fields. Today, Company E is using the power of wireless, broadband and the internet to deliver embedded chip system level and end-to-end network communication solutions for the individual, work team, vehicle and home.

Control

Company E is a US owned organization. All management systems are controlled from its centralized corporate office and a dedicated person, the crisis management vice-president, heads a separate risk management department responsible for monitoring the EHS system (EHS) worldwide. Environmental risk is taken seriously by the organization; it is one of the six corporate objectives on the high priority list.

The controls for the efficient running of the EHS are devised by corporate office based on the guidelines and principles laid down by the ISO standards. Managers accept the organizational objectives and targets of the business plan and consequently accept the controls that go with achieving these objectives. There are disagreements at times because managers may interpret environmental requirements in different ways. There are often intense discussions on what should be the environmental goals but they are eventually resolved.

Integrated system

The current EHS system is based on ISO 14001 and health and safety are incorporated into this system. The three main drivers for the introduction of the environmental management system are first, the moral and ethical issues, second, the legal requirements and third, economic, that is greater savings from improved efficiency for operating processes, waste and energy reduction.

Having an integrated EHS system as opposed to separated environmental and health and safety systems means there is less complexity. The administration of the system (procedures and documentation) is standardized. The corporate auditing team are multi-skilled and audit the EHS system as a whole and not, for example, the environmental or health and safety elements of it. All elements of the EHS system are linked to the business goals and all managers and directors have to approve these goals. Operational goals are manufacturing related and within these goals the environmental, quality and health and safety objectives are clearly specified and accepted by everyone as being part of daily operational activities.

Management commitment and resources

The positioning of a dedicated senior corporate manager for the EMS is seen as necessary to ensure that sufficient resources are made available to support the EMS. A large team of corporate professionals is available to monitor and audit the EHS. Originally each site had its own regional corporate audit team, however, these were centralized to improve efficiency and standardize auditing activity.

Individual sites still have autonomy in running their own EHS systems but it is the site services manager, not the environmental manager, who has responsibility for managing the environment, health and safety, and the facilities. No one in the organization is designated 'environmental manager'.

The organizational structure supports the development of the EHS; there is a clear line of environmental management and clearly defined responsibilities from the top all the way down. As one of the key corporate objectives, environmental management has the support of all managers and directors. It is accepted that EHS support is not wholly prescriptive and that managers and directors do exercise some element of interpretation as to the level of support required.

There is a general view that the operation and development of the EHS is well resourced, although at present there is a requirement for a further two environmental and two health and safety personnel.

Communication

The biggest issue for the organization as regards the EHS is communication. There are 3200 employees within the organization and the majority of these employees work on a shift basis. There are four shifts and keeping everyone informed is a major task and one that is still not fully effective.

There are continuous EHS training programmes that are made available to ensure environmental communication and awareness are maintained. All managers commit to the programme by allocating time for all employees to attend the programmes. Monthly meetings are held by small teams from each shift to review objectives and successes, and this information is fed back to each shift. Weekly audits are undertaken across the four shifts to ensure that the communication and awareness activities are integrated into daily operational activities.

It is the integration of the EHS into daily operational activities that makes the environmental management development plans credible and acceptable. When interviewed, the facilities manager suggested that an integrated approach ensured that 'employee environmental awareness and responsibilities were not additional burdens but were part of a normal working day.'

People are encouraged to approach management to propose change. Open days and company newsletters are used as vehicles to express views for environmental change.

Innovation

Innovation is seen as an important part of keeping the EMS fresh. It is also the hardest area to implement. Environmental goals and objectives are used to introduce innovative ideas into the system, the facilities manager stated that for him:

> The hard part is getting people to participate, awareness levels are high but the hard part is getting people involved, constant communication is required to feedback the successes of innovative ideas. We have a saying here, 'everyone comes here with two arms and two legs and they are entitled to go home with the same'; it is our responsibility to make sure this happens. We have to innovate to keep everything fresh.

Incentives

While continual cost savings are beneficial, making environmental issues part of daily operational activities provides an early warning system for identifying potential environmental incidents. 'We have had no prosecutions on site to date,' said the site facilities manager, but added 'that's not to say there haven't been incidents, there have, but they have been identified early and dealt with.'

The current incentive and reward schemes act as big incentives towards continual environmental improvement. There is keen competition between sites on environmental performance outcomes. Trips to the US are on offer to those individuals or teams that excel in environmental or health and safety improvements. A dedicated corporate team affectionately referred to as the 'MET Office' (Company E ergonomic team), is a multidisciplinary team of 12 members that assess improvements and recommend the rewards. Direct financial incentives are also available and are assessed through the employee appraisal system.

Barriers

The site facilities manager identified two key factors as impeding EHS development. First, the centralized auditing team have overall expertise in monitoring the EHS but at site level there is a tendency to generalize environmental issues and therefore a danger of intimate knowledge of site processes being diminished or lost, thereby increasing the risk of an environmental incident. Second, inconsistent commitment to internal EHS public relations can have an impact. The site facilities manager believes that 'this fluctuates between good and could be better, but it is important to maintain high awareness and training levels to ensure continued management and employee commitment.' He noted that the organization recognizes that local community development is crucial to the continued success of the company. High commitment is given to free local environmental training and education to pupils and students. Due to current economic uncertainties, some of the educational projects are on hold but the task of reassuring the community is a top priority.

Current economic situation
Due to the downturn in the telecommunications sector Company E announced that their forecasts for mobile phone sales in particular were running ahead of consumer demand (Business AM, 2001). A week before the interview unofficial rumours indicated that several thousand jobs at the Bathgate facility could be lost. On the day of the interview I parked my car in an empty car park that would normally have held about 2000 cars. Due to the intense press speculation at the time I was searched for any hidden cameras or recording equipment prior to entering the building. I needed special clearance to use my dictaphone to record the interview. The interview was conducted in an office facility that would normally accommodate several hundred people, yet now there were just two, the site facilities manager and me. The situation was bordering on the surreal but the site facilities manager was still working and so was the integrated EHS system.

Integrated EMS profile

By selecting the key characteristics of the Company E case study, the following profile is that of an organization with an integrated EMS. As integrated system or EHS, is part of daily operational activity. It has one management information system with corporate environmental objectives that are part of the business plan and agreed by all directors and managers. There are good incentive and reward schemes for new environmental initiatives and the integrated system expands and contracts with level of business activity.

Case study of integrated model: Company F

Background
Company F was founded in February 1982 with backing from venture capitalists and has since broken many US business growth records. In 1984 Company F

Table 5.9   *Integrated profile of Company E*

Characteristics of Company E: Integrated EMS	The organization has an accredited EMS
Organizational Drivers	To remain competitive
	Improve efficiency
	Minimize environmental risk
Operational Advantages	Early warning of potential environmental incidents
	Improved efficiency
Operational Disadvantages	Size of company and shift work slows environmental communication
	Decentralized auditing system that causes the loss of site process environmental knowledge
Organizational Barriers	Slow communication channels
	Lack of employee participation
	Management interpretations of environmental requirements
	Lack of IT development

reported first year revenues of US$111.2 million. In 1986 it reported third year revenues of US$503.9 million and shipped its 500,000th personal computer. In 1999 Company F announced that it had shipped over 50 million personal computers in its history.

Interview

Company F's Scottish manufacturing plant was the first site in the Company F corporation to achieve an accredited EMS. They achieved certification for ISO 14001 in August 1998 after a two-year implementation process. The site facilities manager who was interviewed had not installed the existing ISO 14001 system but had operated the system for the 20 months he had been with the company. Previously he was the environmental manager with another computer company for 10 years and had been involved with implementing their ISO 14001 system. He currently reports to the environmental, health and safety, and security director.

There were two main drivers for the pursuit of this environmental standard: first, to attract and retain large commercial customers by demonstrating an environmental commitment demanded by such companies as British Telecom, THUS and South West Water; second, to catch up with a competitor who had been awarded the standard in 1995, and to stay ahead of other competitors that had yet to achieve it. Since 1995, ISO 14001 has been classified as a potential discriminator (a significant marketing advantage or disadvantage) by all electronic original equipment manufacturers (OEMs).

The company addresses environmental risk in the same way as 62 other business standards. All of the company's business standards are built into the corporate business plan and all directors and managers agree the business plan objectives.

Resources

Budgets are made available with the directors and managers aware that they must allocate resources to address environmental considerations as and when the situation arises. Each company within the Company F organization is assessed on these business standards, although the Scotland-based company is the only company that has so far achieved the environmental standards. The assumption is that the Scottish facility manufactures products for Europe and an environmental standard is required if it is to compete effectively. The EHS manager stated that Company F was striving for a worldwide EMS accreditation system and gave IBM as an example of a large electronics organization that began with individually certified EMS sites before moving to corporate EMS accreditation across all its sites. This was considered to be the way forward for Company F.

Culture

The culture of the company is 'States-driven' and everyone from director to shop-floor operator buys-in to the achievement of set targets and objectives and when these are realized they are rewarded for their efforts. Much of the environmental improvement planning is based on specific projects such as waste minimization, energy usage efficiency and material reuse savings. This planning method is seen to have acceptable credibility as managers and employees are rewarded as the company reduces costs.

Communication

The achievement of environmental objectives is communicated well to all employees through using the internet and intranet systems. Details of efficiency savings are issued monthly on spreadsheets that are posted on to the environmental intranet website. Soft copies of ISO 14001 procedures and work instructions together with quality and health and safety procedures are also available for individual inspection. The website has the facility for all employees to offer environmental improvement suggestions.

Innovation

The generation of innovative ideas is encouraged through departmental 'brain storming' sessions and good ideas are communicated throughout the company.

The environmental website is treated as a newsletter and is accessible by all employees through their desktop PCs. Keeping control over the number of innovative ideas for environmental improvement was seen by the EHS manager as the main challenge. He found that 'individual enthusiasm sometimes needed to be restrained or better integrated.' Reference was made to those employees who unilaterally devise and implement their own environmental projects.

Strategy complexity

Compared to its main competitor, Company F management systems are not considered complex because they are treated as one system. All procedures are on the same database and address environmental, quality and health and safety issues within the same procedure. By way of contrast, their main competitor's system is complex, with three separate systems operating in three different business units with three different environmental managers.

System integration

Because the EMS is an integrated part of Company F's overall business management system, this leads to difficulties of control; particularly of EHS external auditing requirements. The BSI certified Company F for ISO 14001 and was also tasked with the periodic (annual) audit of the system. One major requirement of keeping the ISO 14001 standard is a minuted annual management review of the EMS. The fully integrated system operated by Company F was reviewed by senior managers on a 'business plan objectives achieved' process and not the ISO 14001 specified management review basis. After much discussion Company F managed to convince BSI that the annual review of the business plan serves the same function as the management review. This dispensation was also extended to include the ISO 9001 quality standard.

The fully integrated EMS was well received by all managers and directors. One key benefit is that the management systems, environmental, quality and health and safety can be audited by one cross-trained corporate auditing team. The corporate auditing is very effective ensuring that periodic audits are carried out as and when required for each system.

One noticeable drawback to a fully integrated management system is that coordination of the auditing team was led by the corporate quality manager based in the US. The EHS manager said that:

> it was becoming apparent that there was a lack of in-depth knowledge of specific sites, particularly on particular processes and their potential environmental impact. A site-based auditor, with in-depth knowledge of processes, services and products could control more effectively the frequency and the focus of environmental audits. There is a

> *requirement for site-based EHS managers to drive the environmental*
> *management system and to continually educate and train staff both on*
> *a formal and informal basis.*

The current structure of the company is designed so that the company as a whole reports to the US with one integrated management system and one business focus helps the development and the functioning of the EHS. There is a proposal at the discussion stage to split the site into four main business divisions. The existing Company F site will be home to four independent business centres (tandem, commercial desktops, consumer desktops and servers) that report directly via their own business directors to corporate head office in the US. It is feared that this change of structure will fragment the existing EHS system and create four separate environmental, quality, and health and safety systems.

Management commitment

The assumption is that each business director will have their own set of objectives and that environmental issues may not have as high priority as at present. There is also a danger of information being lost between divisions and that available resources will be spread too thinly. At present business and environmental trade-offs are minimal due to everyone having the same business plan objectives to be achieved. Four business units under one roof may require greater trade-offs between the EHS managers and the business unit directors.

One of the criticisms of the existing EHS system is that bureaucracy is still too high. Although all procedures are stored and referenced on the intranet, physical signatures are still required on 'hard' copies that are delivered by hand.

Follow-up interview

Company F was originally interviewed, and their EMS assessed, when there were strong economic conditions in the telecommunications and electronics sector. An opportunity arose to interview the organization following a downturn in this industry sector. It was felt that a follow-up interview would provide insight into whether the model remained consistent in negative economic conditions.

The interview was undertaken by telephone with the same person – the site facilities manager. It was unstructured with the interviewee asked to recall the original interview conversation, to compare the previous situation with the current and to comment on the aspects of the economic downturn. The participant was asked to describe the economic changes that the organization was currently experiencing and to identify any factors that were having an effect on the EHS.

The site facilities manager stated that the EHS remained as one integrated unit incorporating environment, quality and health and safety. The organization was in the process of making 1100 of its 3200 workforce redundant and at the Erskine site, where personal computers were made, the manufacturing process was being moved to the Czech Republic. This process was to be complete by October 2001. At Company F's other Scottish site in Ayr (manufacturing mainframe computers and employing 1500 people) profits remain high and there are no plans for redundancies. This site has the same EHS system as the one applied in Erskine and it remains unchanged.

With the economic downturn Company F's business model has changed. The emphasis is now on high value, low volume products such as mainframes and servers. To achieve this change fewer staff are required as the build process is less intensive. The whole business is being downsized. The EHS is also being downsized but in proportion to the entire organization. Key people are being lost in many departments including three in the EHS department. The EHS manager believes that 'as the organizational manufacturing activities shrink so will the EHS but the administrative and reporting responsibilities will remain but will fit the resized organization.'

Due to the ongoing redundancies and redeployments, it is envisaged that a new awareness and educational programme will need to be undertaken. The timing of new environmental initiatives is important. At the moment there are many sensitive issues within the organization that are taking priority over everything else. For instance, some departments are due environmental audits but these have been cancelled as many employees are unsure whether they will remain with the organization.

As a result of the downsizing, the main barrier acting against the EHS is the lack of commitment from employees as well as managers. Managers' attentions are taken up with the redundancy issues and cost reductions. Employee attentions are taken with the uncertainties of who will be made redundant and looking for alternative employment. This lack of commitment is expected to be short term, possibly six months.

The speed of change is also resulting in poor communications. As the whole organization is downsizing so many messages are being transmitted, some are being misunderstood and some are not received. The speed of communication cannot keep pace with the speed of organizational change and consequently changes to the EHS. As managers are being given increased responsibility they are required to take on several roles, some with conflicting objectives.

While the administration function, although downsized, remains unaffected, participation from other managers has fallen off and internal audits have been scheduled less frequently and environmental meetings for the time being have been stopped. These are considered short-term symptoms and it is anticipated that the normal functioning of the EHS system will resume when the redundancy programme has been completed.

Table 5.10   *Integrated profile of Company F*

Characteristics of Company F: Integrated EMS	The organization has an accredited EMS.
Organizational Drivers	Improve efficiency.
	Minimize environmental risk.
	To remain competitive.
Operational Advantages	Improved efficiency.
	Early warning of potential environmental incidents.
Operational Disadvantages	Size of company and shift work slows environmental communication.
	Decentralized auditing system causing a loss of site process environmental knowledge.
Organizational Barriers	Slow communication channels.
	Lack of employee participation.
	Management interpretations of environmental requirements.
	Lack of IT development.

Integrated EMS profile

By selecting the key characteristics of the Company F case study, the following profile is that of an organization with an integrated environmental management system. Like Company E, this integrated system or EHS system is part of daily operational activity. It has one management information system with corporate environmental objectives and these form part of the business plan agreed upon by all directors and managers. There are good incentive and reward schemes for new environmental initiatives and the integrated system expands and contracts with level of business activity.

USE OF DEVOID, ISOLATED, DEVOLVED AND INTEGRATED MODELS

The application and implementation of an EMS into any organization will invariably produce organizational factors that act for and against implementation. The discussion in Chapter 4 and the case studies in this chapter suggest that environmental management models can be used as tools to assist decision-making in three key areas:

1   organizational EMS development;
2   economic change;
3   competitor discriminator.

Organizational EMS development

The literature and case studies demonstrate that there is consistency in the key organizational drivers that motivate the implementation of environmental management systems. Based on organizational driver consistency the application of the models in this chapter can provide management with insight into how an EMS fits with their organization, the barriers that can arise from the model and the associated operational advantages and disadvantages.

To assist management to make informed decisions, it is not enough just to identify the organizational barriers that exist to impede the development of an EMS. The models in this chapter clearly show the type of barriers and the way these manifest themselves differently between models. It is important for management to understand the cause of the barrier and its impact upon the system and the organization in order that the correct remedial action can be taken. For example, communication is a barrier that can be identified in all models and yet management actions to overcome the barrier will vary between models. The devoid model demonstrates that the simple communication of environmental information to employees is lacking, whereas the integrated model points to the need to refresh the existing communication system to maintain levels of awareness and participation.

Economic change

For organizations that need to react quickly to economic change, the models in this chapter offer additional management information as to how the organization and the EMS will react in both strong and weak economic climates. For example, organizations that operate in highly competitive market sectors may consider that the implementation of a devolved model offers greater operational flexibility when adjusting to frequently fluctuating market conditions. The high cost of operating with a devolved model may be justified by retaining operational flexibility.

Competitor discriminator

Those organizations that seek to be market leaders will view environmental management not just as an environmental risk minimization exercise but also as a business growth and competitive advantage opportunity. To this end, an integrated model ensures that environmental issues are part of daily operational activity and despite organizational growth or contraction, the integrated EMS will remain as part of daily business activity.

Identifying the types of models used by competitors or key suppliers will also provide management with a useful discriminator to gauge the level of competitive advantage and the likely reactions of these organizations to changing economic conditions. The competitive advantage gained from an effective EMS does begin and end with the type of model it uses but can also extend to the types of models applied along the organization's supply chain.

Appendix: Examples of Environmental Charters

EXAMPLE 1: CERES PRINCIPLES

Following the Exxon Valdez oil spill in April 1989, one of the first environmental charters created was by the Coalition for Environmentally Responsible Economies (CERES). The CERES Principles were created by a group of influential US environmental groups with the aim of drafting a corporate code of conduct to protect the environment (CERES, 2005). The principles set out by CERES (2005) are given below:

Protection of the biosphere
We will reduce and make continual progress towards eliminating the release of any substances that may cause environmental damage to air, water, or the Earth or its inhabitants. We will safeguard all habitats affected by our operations and will protect open spaces and wilderness, while preserving biodiversity.

Sustainable use of natural resources
We will make sustainable use of renewable natural resources, such as water, soil and forest. We will conserve non-renewable natural resources through efficient use and careful planning.

Reduction and disposal of waste
We will reduce and where possible eliminate waste through source reduction and recycling. All waste will be handled and disposed of through safe and responsible methods.

Energy conservation
We will conserve energy and improve the energy efficiency of our internal operations and of the goods and services we sell. We will make every effort to use environmentally safe and sustainable energy sources.

Risk reduction

We will strive to minimize the environmental, health and safety risks to our employees and the communities in which we operate through safe technologies, facilities and operating procedures, and by being prepared for emergencies.

Safe products and services

We will reduce and where possible eliminate the use, manufacture or sale of products and services that cause environmental damage or health or safety hazards. We will inform our customers of the environmental impacts of our products or services and try to correct unsafe use.

Environmental restoration

We will promptly and responsibly correct conditions that we have caused that endanger health, safety or the environment. To the extent feasible, we will redress injuries we have caused to persons or damage we have caused to the environment and will restore the environment.

Informing the public

We will inform in a timely manner anyone who may be affected by conditions caused to by our company that might endanger health, safety or the environment. We will regularly seek advice and counsel through dialogue with persons in communities near our facilities. We will not take any action against employees for reporting dangerous incidents or conditions to management or to appropriate authorities.

Management commitment

We will implement these basic principles and sustain a process that ensures that the Board of Directors and Chief Executive Officer are fully informed about pertinent environmental issues and are fully responsible for environmental policy. In selecting our Board of Directors, we will consider demonstrated environmental commitment as a factor.

Audits and reports

We will conduct an annual self-evaluation of our progress in implementing these Principles. We will support the timely creation of generally accepted environmental audit procedures. We will annually complete the CERES Report, which will be made available to the public.

Although commitment to the CERES Principles is voluntary, nearly one hundred companies have signed up (CRT, 2005). Criticisms have been levelled at the Principles. There are no clear definitions or measures as to the amount of 'reduction' of environmental harm. There are no legal obligations to ensure companies comply with the Principles, the effect being that those companies adhering to these Principles need do nothing more than they are doing at the time of signing up. There are no independent audits to ensure that continuous environment improvement is made, which is the one of the cornerstones of sustainable development.

EXAMPLE 2: BUSINESS CHARTER
FOR SUSTAINABLE DEVELOPMENT

A more widely supported charter is the Business Charter for Sustainable Development. Its aim is to help businesses around the world improve their environmental performance and was created by the International Chamber of Commerce. It comprises 16 principles for environmental management that, for business, are a vitally important aspect of sustainable development (ICC, 2005). The principles outlined on the ICC website (2005) are given below:

Corporate priority
To recognize environmental management as among the highest corporate priorities and as a key determinant to sustainable development; to establish policies, programmes and practices for conducting operations in an environmentally sound manner.

Integrated management
To integrate these policies, programmes and practices fully into each business as an essential element of management in all its functions.

Process of improvement
To continue to improve corporate policies, programmes and environmental performance, taking into account technical developments, scientific understanding, consumer needs and community expectations, with legal regulations as a starting point; and to apply the same environmental criteria internationally.

Employee education
To educate, train and motivate employees to conduct their activities in an environmentally responsible manner.

Prior assessment

To assess environmental impacts before starting a new activity or project and before decommissioning a facility or leaving a site.

Products and services

To develop and provide products or services that have no undue environmental impact and are safe in their intended use, that are efficient in their consumption of energy and natural resources, and that can be recycled, reused, or disposed of safely.

Customer advice

To advise, and where relevant educate, customers, distributors and the public in the safe use, transportation, storage and disposal of products provided; and to apply similar considerations to the provision of services.

Facilities and operations

To develop, design and operate facilities and conduct activities taking into consideration the efficient use of energy and materials, the sustainable use of renewable resources, the minimization of adverse environmental impact and waste generation, and the safe and responsible disposal of residual wastes.

Research

To conduct or support research on the environmental impacts of raw materials, products, processes, emissions and wastes associated with the enterprise and on the means of minimizing such adverse impacts.

Precautionary approach

To modify the manufacture, marketing or use of products or services or the conduct of activities, consistent with scientific and technical understanding, to prevent serious or irreversible environmental degradation.

Contractors and suppliers

To promote the adoption of these principles by contractors acting on behalf of the enterprise, encouraging and, where appropriate, requiring improvements in their practices to make them consistent with those of the enterprise; and to encourage the wider adoption of these principles by suppliers.

Emergency preparedness

To develop and maintain, where significant hazards exist, emergency preparedness plans in conjunction with the emergency services, relevant authorities and the local community, recognizing potential transboundary impacts.

Transfer of technology

To contribute to the transfer of environmentally sound technology and management methods throughout the industrial and public sectors.

Contributing to the common effort

To contribute to the development of public policy and to business, governmental and intergovernmental programmes and educational initiatives that will enhance environmental awareness and protection.

Openness to concerns

To foster openness and dialogue with employees and the public, anticipating and responding to their concerns about the potential hazards and impacts of operations, products, wastes or services, including those of transboundary or global significance.

Compliance and reporting

To measure environmental performance; to conduct regular environmental audits and assessments of compliance with company requirements, legal requirements and these principles; and periodically to provide appropriate information to the Board of Directors, shareholders, employees, the authorities and the public.

Support for the Charter

The ICC undertakes to encourage member companies and others to express their support and implement the Charter and its principles. A list of these companies can be obtained from ICC Headquarters. The ICC also regularly publishes a Charter bulletin, which provides more specific information on the Charter's principles and different interpretations possible – an attribute of the Charter that has been widely commended.

The Business Charter for Sustainable Development provides a basic framework of reference for action by individual corporations and business organizations throughout the world. It has been recognized as a complement to environmental management systems. To this end, the ICC, the United Nations Environment Programme (UNEP) and the

International Federation of Consulting Engineers (FIDIC) have developed a kit to help enterprises integrate EMS in daily management practices, a step consistent with the objectives set out in this Charter. The Business Charter has been published in over 20 languages, including all the official languages of the United Nations.

Example 3: Chemical industries association – responsible care guiding principles

The first and most demanding of the qualifying requirements is that a member company, at chief executive level, commits itself to adhere to the Responsible Care Guiding Principles. These are set out by the Sustainable Development Pioneers Group (2005) as follows:

This company manages all aspects of its activities so that we provide a high level of protection for the health and safety of employees and associates, customers, and the public; and for the environment. We will demonstrate our commitment to sustainable development and continual improvement by adhering to the following principles:

Policy
We will have a Health, Safety and Environmental (HS&E) policy, which will reflect our commitment and be an integral part of our overall business policy.

Employee involvement
We recognize that the involvement and commitment of our employees and associates will be essential to the achievement of our objectives. We will adopt communication and training programmes aimed at achieving that involvement and commitment.

Experience sharing
In addition to ensuring our activities meet the relevant statutory obligations, we will share experience with our industry colleagues and seek to learn from and incorporate best practice into our own activities.

Legislators and regulators
We will seek to work in cooperation with legislators and regulators.

Process safety
We will assess and manage the risks associated with our processes.

Product stewardship
We will assess the risks associated with our products, and seek to ensure these risks are properly managed throughout the supply chain through stewardship programmes involving our customers, suppliers and distributors.

Resource conservation
We will work to conserve resources and reduce waste in all our activities.

Stakeholder engagement
We will monitor our HS&E performance and report progress to stakeholders; we will listen to the appropriate communities and engage them in dialogue about our activities and our products.

Management systems
We will maintain documented management systems which are consistent with the Principles of Responsible Care and which will be subject to a formal verification procedure.

Past, present and future
Our Responsible Care management systems will address the impact of both current and past activities.

EXAMPLE 4: ENVIRONMENTAL CHARTER OF EUROPEAN TELECOMMUNICATION NETWORK OPERATORS (ETNO)

Vision

Sustainable development is a strategic global environmental goal. It describes development that takes into consideration the need to conserve both the natural environment and the world's scarce non-renewable resources for future generations. It is our belief that we can play an important part in making this happen.

This Charter describes our commitment to sustainable development through the provision of products and services that provide significant environmental benefits a determination to manage our own operations in a way that minimizes negative environmental impacts.

The ETNO recognizes that the universal presence of telecommunications in today's society places on us a social obligation to be good corporate citizens. A responsible attitude to environmental issues is an important part of meeting that obligation. As a collective group of companies, our combined turnover represents a significant proportion of European trade and this puts us in a unique position to make a real difference.

ETNO is committed to continuous improvement through action in the following areas:

- *Awareness: We shall aim to ensure recognition and acknowledgement of all relevant environmental impacts, including the positive and negative impacts of our products and services. In particular we shall build the environment into our training programmes and company communication programmes.*
- *Regulatory compliance: We shall strive to achieve full compliance with all relevant environmental legal requirements, and to exceed these requirements where appropriate.*
- *Research and development: We shall support research and development into the contribution new telecommunication services can make to sustainable development.*
- *Procurement: We shall build environmental considerations into our procurement processes. Special attention will be paid to: energy-consumption, waste management, process and product requirements, the use of hazardous materials.*
- *Providing information: We shall provide relevant data and information about our environmental performance to employees, customers, shareholders and governments.*
- *Environmental management systems: We shall implement environmental management systems, which support the development of appropriate and well-structured environmental protection.* (ETNO, 2005)

EXAMPLE 5: EUROPEAN PETROLEUM INDUSTRY ASSOCIATION

The European Petroleum Industry Association (EUROPIA) was founded in 1989 and is located in Brussels. It currently has 26 members ranging from multinational corporations to national operators. The aims of the association are to contribute to the study and solution of issues arising from the manufacture, marketing and use of petroleum products in terms of quality control, environmental protection and health and safety. It also gives its view on proposed regulations or directives of the European Community concerning the downstream oil industry to promote understanding of the oil industry's contribution to economic, technological and social progress with the general public and public authorities.

The main activities of EUROPIA arise from energy policy, protection of the environment and product quality. Specific current issues are:

- auto-oil programmes;
- air quality directives;
- acidification strategy;
- climate change;
- economic issues;
- competition legislation;
- EU enlargement.

Membership of EUROPIA is open to companies who own and/or operate mineral oil refining facilities in the European Union. EUROPIA members operate some 95 per cent of the total EU oil refining capacity .

EXAMPLE 6: JAPANESE SHIPOWNERS' ASSOCIATION ENVIRONMENTAL CHARTER

The Japanese Shipowners' Association (JSA), recognizing the importance of conserving the earth and the marine environment as being among the highest priorities, seeks for perfection in the safe navigation of vessels as well as promoting the easing of burdens on the environment and the effective use of resources, with the aim of reducing the risk of sea disasters and oil spills which inevitably cause marine pollution. In escalating its efforts to advance the preservation of the environment, the JSA will at the same time continue to contribute to the healthy development of the Japanese and world economies, in recognition of the shipping industry being an important logistical element of the infrastructure which supports all industrial activities and people's lives.

Action guidelines
- *Having formulated its action guidelines for the conservation of the environment, as listed below, the JSA will promote measures to protect the environment and help member companies with their proactive activities toward environmental preservation.*

- *Further conservation of the environment by strict adherence to domestic and international legislation concerning the earth and marine environment and voluntary implementation of environment-related policies.*
- *Establishment and enforcement of management systems designed to secure the safe navigation of vessels, also support and promotion of the development and installation of equipment to contribute.*
- *Employment of energy-saving, high-efficiency vessels and devices, reduction in the potential environmental impacts generated by vessel operations, and diminution and proper disposal of waste.*
- *Active endorsement of the elimination of sub-standard vessels which cause marine pollution-inducing accidents, and promotion of ship recycling.*
- *Provision of thorough education and training for the purpose of improving vessel navigation skills and conserving the earth and marine environment.*
- *Maintenance of proper systems and facilities so that disasters at sea or other major accidents can be quickly dealt with.*
- *Timely and consistent distribution of information on actions undertaken to preserve the environment and reinforcement of daily activities with a view to raising people's environmental awareness and conserving the environment.*
- *Strengthening of cooperation with relevant organizations in Japan and overseas on environmental issues, and participation in and contribution to both domestic and international forums and conferences. (JSA, 2005)*

Example 7: Environmental Charter of the Southern African Natural Products Trade Association

The Southern African Natural Products Trade Association (SANPRoTA) are committed to promoting the principles of sustainable use and sound environmental management in the production and trade of natural products in the Southern African region and internationally, and are willing to express our commitment through signature to a common Charter:

Product selection
- *Prior to selecting a product, we shall compile a written justification for the selection that specifically details the distribution, abundance and conservation status of the biological resource from which it is derived.*

- *In the selection of natural products, we shall ensure that special care is taken to guarantee the sustainability of biological resources that are comparatively rare, or that occur in fragile or vulnerable ecosystems.*
- *We shall endeavour to ensure that the long-term tenure and use rights to the land and biological resources from which our natural products are derived are clearly defined, documented and legally established.*

Harvesting methods

- *We shall ensure that all harvesting methods used in the production of natural products shall minimize adverse environmental impacts, including, where appropriate, through in situ management, domestication and cultivation.*
- *We shall maintain a written description and justification of harvesting techniques and equipment used.*
- *In our production activities, we shall minimize waste associated with harvesting and on-site processing operations, and avoid negative environmental impacts.*

Resource regeneration

- *We shall endeavour to ensure that, at all times, the rate of harvest of a biological resource shall not exceed levels, which can be sustained.*
- *For each natural product we produce, we shall maintain a written justification of the regenerative capacity of the biological resource from which it is obtained.*

Resource management

- *We shall encourage the development, implementation and monitoring of resource management plans for all biological resources from which our natural products are derived.*
- *In the management of, and harvest from, biological resources, we shall encourage the efficient use of the ecosystem's multiple products and services to ensure economic viability and a wide range of environmental and social benefits.*
- *In our resource management and harvesting activities, we shall conserve biological diversity and its associated values, water resources, soils, and unique and fragile ecosystems and landscapes, and, by so doing, maintain the ecological functions and the integrity of the ecosystem.*

- *Ecological functions and values shall be maintained intact, enhanced, or restored, including:*
  - *regeneration and succession;*
  - *genetic, species, and ecosystem diversity;*
  - *natural cycles that affect the productivity of the ecosystem.*
- *Resource management should strive towards economic viability, while taking into account the full environmental, social, and operational costs of production, and ensuring the investments necessary to maintain the ecological integrity of the ecosystem.*
- *We shall encourage the optimal use and local processing of an ecosystem's diversity of products.*
- *We shall promote the development and adoption of environmentally friendly methods of pest management and strive to avoid the use of any pesticides banned by international agreement. If chemicals are used, proper equipment and training shall be provided to minimize health and environmental risks and chemicals, containers, liquid and solid non-organic wastes including fuel and oil shall be disposed of in an environmentally appropriate manner.*
- *Where we use biological control agents, this shall be documented, minimized, monitored and strictly controlled in accordance with national laws and internationally accepted scientific protocols. We shall not use Genetically Modified Organisms.*
- *The use of exotic species shall be carefully controlled and actively monitored to avoid adverse ecological impacts.*

Compliance with laws
In the production and trade of natural products, we shall respect all applicable laws of the country in which they occur, and any international treaties and agreements to which the country is a signatory (in particular, the Convention on International Trade in Endangered Species, the Convention on Biological Diversity, and the Ramsar Convention on Wetlands).

Tenure and use rights and responsibilities
We shall uphold the principle that local communities with legal or customary tenure or use rights maintain control, to the extent necessary to protect their rights or resources, over the harvesting and manufacture of natural products, unless they delegate control with free and informed consent to other agencies.

Indigenous peoples' rights

- *We shall respect and recognize the legal and customary rights of indigenous peoples to own, use and manage their lands, territories, and resources.*
- *The management and use of biological resources for our products shall not threaten or diminish, either directly or indirectly, the resources or tenure rights of indigenous peoples.*
- *Sites of special cultural, ecological, economic or religious significance to indigenous peoples shall be clearly identified in cooperation with such peoples, and recognized and protected by resource managers.*
- *Indigenous peoples shall be compensated for the application of their traditional knowledge regarding the use of plant species or management systems in our operations. This compensation shall be formally agreed upon with their free and informed consent before such operations commence.*
- *We recognize the complexities surrounding the rights of indigenous peoples in the commercialization of biological resources, and commit ourselves to the development of meaningful and innovative solutions to access and benefit sharing issues.*

EXAMPLE 8: UK OVERSEAS TERRITORIES AND THE ENVIRONMENTAL CHARTER

In 1999, the UK Overseas Territories Conservation Forum (UKOTCF) reported on the early stages of their Environmental Charter process:

> *The year 1998/99 saw major progress on the part of the Forum. We are particularly pleased with the progress made in joint developments with UK Government. From a situation early in 1998 when the Forum had to deplore the lack of attention to the environment in the Government's major policy statement, we have moved to a situation in which the environment forms a major, and widely commended, chapter of the Government's White Paper on the UK Overseas Territories Partnership for Progress and Prosperity, published on the Foreign and Commonwealth site in March 1999.* (UKOTCF, 2005)

In mid-1998, the Forum edited a special edition of Ecos, the journal of the British Association of Nature Conservationists (BANC). This included a range of articles about the UK overseas territories as well as a set of recommendations for the UK government to address in respect of its responsibilities to the environment in its overseas territories (UKOTCF, 2005).

Agreed principles

In late September 2001, environmental charters were signed between UK and UKOTs. The signatories of the charters are:

- Anguilla;
- Ascension;
- Bermuda;
- British Indian Ocean Territory;
- British Virgin Islands;
- Cayman Islands;
- Falkland Islands;
- Montserrat;
- South Georgia and the South Sandwich Islands;
- St Helena;
- Turks and Caicos Islands.

The signed charters are valuable commitments by the governments of the UK and its overseas territories. However, these are just a first element as envisaged by the participants in the Breath of Fresh Air conference and by other stakeholders at that time. Still needed are the strategies or action plans to link these aspirational documents to real progress on the ground. This need was met earlier to some extent by the Conservation Priorities section of the Forum's Conservation Review of 1996. Forum partners in the UK's overseas territories are progressively updating this material (UKOTCF, 2005).

Progress in developing the charts has been slow, with the UK's overseas territories making it clear that resources are essential for progress. They look to the similar process initiated by the Organization of Eastern Caribbean States (OECS) that is progressing more effectively due to OECS resources facilitation. UK overseas territories have indicated repeatedly (for example at the Gibraltar conference) that similar facilitation is needed to assist people in the territories to develop their own action plans, an integral part of the UK Environmental Charter. They have welcomed the Forum's indication that it could help provided that costs could be covered. The UK Foreign and Commonwealth Office (FCO) has asked the Forum to provide facilitation, but between 1999 and 2002, a mechanism could not be found to provide the modest resources committed under the signed charters.

EXAMPLE 9: WORLD BUSINESS COUNCIL
FOR SUSTAINABLE DEVELOPMENT

The World Business Council for Sustainable Development (WBCSD) is a coalition of 160 international companies united by a shared commitment to sustainable development via the three pillars of economic growth, ecological balance and social progress. Members are drawn from more than 30 countries and 20 major industrial sectors. The WBCSD also benefits from a global network of 40 national and regional business councils and partner organizations, involving some 1000 business leaders globally. The WBCSD was formed in January 1995 through a merger between the Business Council for Sustainable Development (BCSD) in Geneva and the World Industry Council for the Environment (WICE) in Paris. Since then the WBCSD has become the pre-eminent business voice on sustainable development issues, playing a leading role in shaping business's response to the challenges of sustainable development. The council outlines (WBCSD, 2005) its mission and objectives as follows:

WBCSD mission
To provide business leadership as a catalyst for change toward sustainable development, and to promote the role of eco-efficiency, innovation and corporate social responsibility.

Aims
To be the leading business advocate on issues connected with sustainable development.

Policy development
To participate in policy development in order to create a framework that allows business to contribute effectively to sustainable development.

Best practice
To demonstrate business progress in environmental and resource management and corporate social responsibility and to share leading-edge practices among our members.

Global outreach
To contribute to a sustainable future for developing nations and nations in transition.

Governance
WBCSD is a member-led organization governed by a Council composed of the Chief Executive Officers of its member companies, or other top-level executives of equivalent rank. It meets annually to

decide the organization's priorities and to discuss strategic issues connected with sustainable development. These Council meetings provide a forum where business leaders can analyse, debate and exchange experiences on all aspects of sustainable development.

References

Ackroyd, J., Coulter, B., Phillips, P. and Read, A. (2003) 'Business excellence through resource efficiency (betre): An evaluation of the UK's highest recruiting, facilitated self-help waste minimization project', *Resources, Conservation and Recycling*, vol 38, pp271–299

Acorn Trust (2005) 'Phased implementation: How does it work?', www.theacorntrust. org/in_method_intro.shtml

Ammenberg, J. and Sundin, E. (2005) 'Products in environmental management systems: Drivers, barriers and experiences', *Journal of Cleaner Production*, vol 13, pp405–415

Ansoff, H.I. (1991) 'Critique of Henry Mintzbergs *The Design School: Reconsidering One Basic Premises of Strategic Management*', *Strategic Management Journal*, vol 12, pp449–61

Argyris, C. (1993) *Knowledge for Action*, Jossey-Bass, San Francisco

Australian Department of the Environment and Heritage (2005) 'Greenhouse Challenge Plus, Staff Success Story', www.greenhouse.gov.au/challenge/tools/staff_success _stories.html

Avila, J. A. and Whitehead, B. W. (1993) 'What is environmental strategy?', *The McKinsey Quarterly*, vol 4, pp53–68

Azzone, G. and Bertelè, U. (1994) 'Exploiting green strategies for competitive advantage', *Long Range Planning*, vol 27, pp69–81

Azzone, G., Bertelè, U. and Noci, G. (1997) 'At last we are creating environmental strategies which work', *Long Range Planning*, vol 30, pp478–571

Ball J. (2002) 'Can ISO 14000 and eco-labelling turn the construction industry green?', *Building and Environment*, vol 37, no 4, pp421–428

Ball, S. and Bell, S. (1997) *Environmental Law*, Blackstone Press, London

Banerjee, S. B. (2002) 'Corporate environmentalism: the construct and its measurement', *Journal of Business Research*, vol 55, no 3, pp177–191

Beaumont, J. R. (1992) 'Managing the environment: Business opportunity and responsibility', *Futures*, April, pp187–205

Boeker, W. (1997) 'Strategic change: The influences of managerial characteristics and organizational growth', *Academy of Management Journal*, vol 40, no 1, pp152–170

British Standards Institute (1992) *BS 7750 Specification for Environmental Management Systems*, BSI, Milton Keynes

Business AM (2001) *Business AM*, daily newspaper, 14 March, p1

Business For Social Responsibility Education Fund (2001), 'Suppliers' Perspectives on Greening the Supply Chain-A report on suppliers' views on effective supply chain environmental management strategies', www.getf.org/file/toolmanager/O16F15429 .pdf

Buzzelli, D. T. (1991) 'Time to structure an environmental policy strategy', *Journal of Business* Strategy, March/April, pp17–20

Carson, R. (1962) *Silent Spring*, Houghton Mifflin, New York

Castledine, J. (2001) 'Pollution prevention and Responsible Care®: Dow's recipe for success', *International Conference on Cleaner Production*, Beijing, China, www.chinacp.com/eng/cpconfer/iccp01/iccp40.html

Caulkin, S. (2003) 'Milk of corporate kindness', *The Observer*, London, 23 November

CEN (1997) *CEN Report CR 12969*, European Committee for Standardization, Brussels

CERES (2005) 'The CERES Principles', www.ceres.org/

Charter, M. (1992) *Greener Marketing*, Sheffield, Greenleaf Publishing

Charter, M., Kielkiewicz-Young, A., Young A. and Hughes A. (2001) 'Supply Chain Strategy and Evaluation Case Studies', www.projectsigma.com/RnDStreams/RD_supply_chain_case.pdf

Child, J. A. (1972) *Organization: A Guide to Problems and Practice*, Harper & Row, London

Cochin, T. J. (1998) 'Continuously improving your environmental strategies', *Corporate Environmental Strategy*, vol 5, no 2, pp57–60

Cohen, W. M. and Levinthal, D. A. (1990) 'Absorptive capacity: A new perspective on learning and innovation', *Administrative Science Quarterly*, vol 35, pp128–152

Commission of The European Communities (CEC) (1993) *Official Journal of the European Communities*, L168/1–18, July

Corbett, C. J. and Wassenhove, L. N. (1993) 'The green fee: Internalising and operationalising environmental issues', *California Management Review*, Fall, pp116–135

Cramer, J. and Zegveld, W. C. L. (1991) 'The future role of technology in environmental management', *Futures*, June, pp451–468

CRT (2005) 'CERES Principles', The Caux Round Table, www.cauxroundtable.org/CERESPrinciples.html

Currie, J. (1993) 'An approach to assessing the management of environmental responsibilities in federal departments and agencies', *The Journal of Public Sector Management*, September, pp69–77

Dodge, H. and Welford, R. (1995) 'The ROAST Scale' in R. Welford (ed) *Corporate Environmental Management: Systems and Strategies*, Earthscan, London, pp21–22

Eagen, D. and Streckewald, K. E. (1997) 'Striving to improve business success through increased environmental awareness and design for the environment education case study: AMP Incorporated', *Journal of Cleaner Production*, vol 5, no 3, pp219–223

Eisenhardt, K. M. (1989) 'Building theories from case study research', *Academy of Management Review*, vol 14, no 4, pp532–550

Elkington, J. and Hailes, J. (1987) *The Green Consumer Guide: High Street Shopping for a Better Environment*, Victor Gollancz, London

ENDS Report (2005a) 'First ever IPPC prosecution for noise pollution', *ENDS Report*, vol 362, p 59

ENDS Report (2005b) 'Foundry fined £45,000 for fume emission', *ENDS Report*, vol 363, p 61

ENDS Report (2005c) 'Solvent leak costs waste firm £27,000', *ENDS Report*, vol 363, p 61

ETNO (2005) 'The Sustainability Charter of the European Telecommunications Network Operators' Association', European Telecommunications Network Operators' Association, www.etno.be/upload/down_files/9354/Sustainability%20Charter.doc

EUROPIA (2005) 'Environmental guiding principles', European Petroleum Industry Association, www.europia.com/HTML/Europia.htm

Floyd, S. W. and Wooldridge, B. (1992) 'Managing strategic consensus: The foundation of effective implementation', *Academy of Management Executive*, vol 6, no 4, pp27–39

Foster, C. and Green, K. (2000) 'Greening the innovation process', *Business Strategy and the Environment*, vol 9, no 5, pp287–303

Fuller, M. K. and Swanson, E. B. (1992) 'Information centres as organizational innovation: Exploring the correlates of implementation success', *Journal of Management Information Systems*, vol 9, no 1, pp47–67

Gallarotti, G. M. (1995) 'It pays to be green', *The Columbia Journal of World Business*, Winter, pp38–57

Gascoigne, J. (2002) 'Supply chain management – Project Acorn', *Corporate Environmental Strategy*, vol 9, no 1, pp62–68

González-Benito, J. and González-Benito, O. (2005) 'A study of the motivation for the environmental transformation of companies', *Industrial Marketing Management*, vol 34, pp462–475

Greeno, J. L. (1991) 'Environmental excellence: Meeting the challenge', *Arthur D. Little Prism*, Third Quarter, pp13–31

Greeno, J. L. and Robinson, S. N. (1992) 'Rethinking corporate environmental management', *The Columbia Journal of World Business*, Fall and Winter, pp223– 232

Greiner, L. E. (1972) 'Evolution and revolution as organizations grow', *Harvard Business Review*, July/August, pp37–46

Hale, M. (1995) 'Training for environmental technologies and environmental management', *Journal of Cleaner Production*, vol 3, nos 1–2, pp19–23

Hart, S. L. (1997) 'Beyond greening: Strategies for a sustainable world', *Harvard Business Review*, January/February, pp66–76

Haveman, M. and Dorfman, M. (1999) 'Breaking down the "green wall" (part one): Early efforts at integrating business and environment at SC Johnson', *Corporate Environmental Strategy*, vol 6, no 1, pp5–13

Hillary, R. (2004) 'Environmental management systems and the smaller enterprise', *Journal of Cleaner Production*, vol 12, pp561–569

Hui, I. K., Chan, A. H. S., Pun, K. F. (2001) 'A study of the environmental management system implementation practices', *Journal of Cleaner Production*, vol 9, pp269–276

Hunt, C. B. and Auster, E. A. (1990) 'Proactive environmental management: Avoiding the toxic trap', *Sloan Management Review*, Winter, pp7–18

Hutchinson, C. (1996) 'Integrating environmental policy with business strategy', *Long Range Planning*, vol 29, no 1, pp11–23

ICC (1994) 'Principles of Environmental Management', summary report of ICC seminar, London, International Chamber of Commerce

ICC (2005) 'The Business Charter for Sustainable Development', International Chamber of Commerce, www.iccwbo.org/home/environment_and_energy/charter.asp

Irwin, A., Georg, S. and Vergragt, P. (1994) 'The social management of environmental change', *Futures*, vol 26, no 3, pp323–334

JSA (2005) 'JSA Environmental Charter', Japanese Shipowners' Association, www.jsanet.or.jp/e/enviro-e/

Kantz, O. (2000) 'Volvo's holistic approach to environmental strategy', *Corporate Environmental Strategy*, vol 7, pp156–169

Khanna, M. and Anton W. R. Q. (2002) 'What is driving corporate environmentalism: opportunity or threat?', *Corporate Environmental Strategy*, vol 9, no 4, pp409–417

Kirkland, L. H. and Thompson, D. (1999) 'Challenges in designing, implementing and operating an environmental management system', *Business Strategy and the Environment*, vol 8, pp128–143

Kleiner, A. (1991) 'What does it mean to be green?', *Harvard Business Review*, July/August, pp38–47

Kolk, A. and Mauser, A. (2002) 'The evolution of environmental management: From stage models to performance evaluation', *Business Strategy and the Environment*, vol 11, pp14–31

Kotsmith, J. (2004) 'The Next Generation of Pollution Prevention Pays (3P) at 3M', presentation given at the National Environmental Assistance Summit, www.p2.org/summit2004/documents/Presentations/Kotsmith%20James.ppt

Lee, B. W. and Green, K. (1994) 'Towards commercial and environmental excellence: A green portfolio matrix', *Business Strategy and the Environment*, vol 3, no 3, pp1–9

Local Government Management Board (1991) *Environmental Auditing in Local Government*, Luton, LGMB

Lorsch, J. and Allen, S. (1973) *Managing Diversity and Independence*, Harvard University Press, Cambridge, MA.

McBoyle, G. (1996) 'Green tourism and Scottish distilleries', *Tourism Management*, vol 17, no 4, pp255–263

McGrew, A. (1990) 'The political dynamics of the new environmentalism', *Industrial Crisis Quarterly*, vol 4, pp292–305

Melnyk, S. A., Sroufe, R. P. and Calantone, R. (2003) 'Assessing the impact of environmental management systems on corporate and environmental performance', *Journal of Operations Management*, vol 21, no 3, pp329–351

Miles, R. E. and Snow, C. C. (1978) *Organization, Strategy and Structure*, McGraw-Hill, Emeryville, CA

Miller, D. and Freisen, P. H. (1980) 'Momentum and revolution in organizational adaptation', *Academy of Management Journal*, vol 23, pp591–614

Mintzberg, H. (1987) 'Crafting Strategy', *Harvard Business Review*, July/August, pp38–47

Morrow, D. and Rondinelli, D. (2002) 'Adopting corporate environmental management systems: Motivations and results of ISO 14001 and EMAS certification', *European Management Journal*, vol 20, no 2, pp159–171

Müller, K. and Koechlin, D. (1992) *Green Bushess Opportunities: The Profit Potential*, Pitman, London

Patel, P. and Younger, M. (1978) 'A frame of reference for strategy development', *Long Range Planning*, vol 11, pp6–12

Pearson, M. (2004) 'Effective waste management brings company £30,000 cost savings', *High Growth Business Network Newsletter*, Yorkshire and Humberside region, www.rtn.co.uk/Hgbn/newsletters/Newsletter%20April%202004.pdf

Peattie, K. J. (1990) 'Painting marketing education (or how to recycle old ideas)', *Journal of Marketing Management*, vol 6, no 2, pp105–125

Peters, T. J. and Waterman, R. H. (1989) *In Search of Excellence: Lessons from America's Best Run Companies*, Harper and Row, New York

Petulla, J. M. (1987) *Environmental Protection in the United States*, San Francisco Study Center, San Francisco, CA

Pfeffer, J. (1996) 'When it comes to "best practices" – why do smart organisations occasionally do dumb things?', *Organisational Dynamics*, summer, pp33–43

Piercy, N. (1989) 'Diagnosing and solving implementation problems in strategic planning', *Journal of General Management*, vol 15, no 1, pp19–38

Porter, M. E. and van der Linde, C. (1992) 'Green and competitive', *Harvard Business Review*, September/October, pp120–134

Prothero, A. (1990) 'Green consumerism and the societal marketing concept marketing strategies for the 1990s', *Journal of Marketing Management*, vol 6, no 2, pp147–166

Prothero, A. and McDonagh, P. (1992) 'Producing environmentally acceptable cosmetics: The impact of environmentalism on the UK cosmetics and toiletries industry', *Journal of Marketing Management*, vol 8, pp147–166

Punjari, D. and Wright, G. (1994) 'Strategic Green Marketing: An Integrated Approach', Marketing Education Group, Annual Conference, University of Ulster, Northern Ireland

Quinn, J. B. (1978) 'Strategic change: Logical incrementalism', *Sloan Management Review*, Fall, pp7–19

Quinn, J. B. (1980) 'Managing strategic change', *Sloan Management Review*, Summer, pp3–20

Ramus, C. A. (1998) 'How environmental communication supports employee participation: A case study of EMI Music', *Corporate Environmental Strategy*, vol 5, no 4, pp69–74

Ramus, C. A. (2002) 'Encouraging innovative environmental actions: What companies and managers must do', *Journal of World Business*, vol 37, pp151–164

Reed, R. and Buckley, M. R. (1988) 'Strategy in action: Techniques for implementing strategy', *Long Range Planning*, vol 21, no 3, pp67–74

Rennings, K., Ziegler, A., Ankele, K. and Hoffmann, E. (forthcoming) 'The influence of different characteristics of the EU Environmental Management and Auditing Scheme on Technical Environmental Innovations and Economic Performance', *Ecological Economics*, article in press, corrected proof

Roome, N. (1992) 'Developing environmental management strategies', *Business Strategy and the Environment*, vol 1, no 1, pp11–24

Roome, N. (1994) 'Business strategy, R&D management and environmental imperatives', *R&D Management*, vol 24, pp65–82

Rothenberg, S., Maxwell, J. and Marcus, A. (1992) 'Issues in the implementation of proactive environmental strategies', *Business Strategy and the Environment*, vol 1, no 4, pp1–12

Schein, E. (1987) *Process Consultation (Volume 2)*, Addison-Wesley, London

Shelton, R. D. (1994) 'Hitting the green wall: Why corporate programmes get stalled', *Corporate Environmental Strategy*, vol 2, no 2, pp5–11

Shimell, P. (1991) 'Corporate environmental policy in practice', *Long Range Planning*, vol 24, no 3, pp10–17

Shrivastava, P. and Hart, S. (1994) 'Greening organizations', *International Journal of Public Administration*, vol 17, nos 3–4, pp607–635

Smith, G. (1990), 'How Green is my Valley', *Marketing and Research Today*, June, pp76–82

Steger, U (1988) *Umweltmanagement, Erfahrungen und Instrumente einer Umweltorientierten Unternehmensstrategie*, Gabler, Wiesbaden

Steger, U. (2000) 'Environmental management systems: Empirical evidence and further perspectives', *European Management Journal*, vol 18, no 1, pp23–37

Stone, L. (2000) 'When case studies are not enough: The influence of corporate culture and employee attitudes on the success of cleaner production initiatives', *Journal of Cleaner Production*, vol 8, pp353–359

Sustainable Development Pioneers Group (2005) 'Sustainable Development Chemical Industries Association Leadership Statement', www.pioneersgroup.co.uk/uploads/stored/CIA%20SD%20Leadership%20Statement.doc

Tapon, F. and Sarabura, M. (1995) 'The greening of corporate strategy in the chemical industry: Two steps forward one step back', *Journal of Strategic Change*, vol 4, pp307–321

Taylor, S. R. (1992) 'Green management: The next competitive weapon', *Futures*, September, pp669–680

Tinsley, S. (2001) *Environmental Management Plans Demystified: A Guide to ISO 14001*, Taylor & Francis, London

Tinsley, S. (2002) 'EMS models for business strategy development', *Business Strategy and the Environment*, vol 11, no 6, pp376–390

Tinsley, S. and Melton, K. (1997) 'Sustainable development and its effect on the marketing planning process', *Eco-Management and Auditing Journal*, vol 4, no 3, pp116–126

Tsai, S. H. T. and Child, J. (1997) 'Strategic responses of multinational corporations to environmental demands', *Journal of General Management*, vol 23, no 1, pp1–21

UKOTCF (2005) 'UK Overseas Territories and the Environmental Charter' UK Overseas Territories Conservation Forum, www.ukotcf.org/charter.htm

Vastag, G., Kerekes, S., Rondinelli, D. (1996) 'Evaluation of corporate environmental management approaches: A framework and application', *International Journal of Production Economics*, vol 43, pp193–211

Walley, N. and Whitehead, B. (1994) 'It's not easy being green', *Harvard Business Review*, May/June, pp46–52

WBCSD (2005) Website of World Business Council for Sustainable Development, http://www.wbcsd.ch/templates/TemplateWBCSD5/layout.asp?MenuID=1

Welford, R. (1996) *Corporate Environmental Management*, Earthscan Publications, London

Welford, R. and Gouldson, A. (1993) *Environmental Management and Business Strategy*, Pitman Publishing, London

Wheeler, D. (1993) '*Building ecological and public attitude concerns into your business strategy*', conference proceedings, World Class Corporate Planning, IIR, 23–25 November, Institute of International Research, Oxford University Press, Oxford

Winn, M. I. and Angell, A. C. (2000) 'Towards a process model of corporate greening', *Organizational Studies*, vol 21, no 6, pp1119–1147

World Commission on Environment and Development (1987) *Our Common Future*, (The Brundtland Report), Oxford University Press, Oxford

Index

3M   4, 5, 9, 94
'3Ps' (Pollution Prevention Pays)   4, 5, 9

absorptive capacity   81, 82
Ackroyd, J.   14
Agyris, C.   81
air pollution   12
analysis matrix   38–41
Angell, A. C.   97
anticipative context   100
anticipatory attitude   87, 88
anticipatory green strategy   94–95
Anton, W. R. Q.   13
aspects and impacts   27, 35–41
audits   15, 25, 27–35
   case studies   136, 143
   eco-management   16–17, 20–21
   evidence   66
   external   28, 32–35
   internal   28–32, 55–56
   notification   64–65
   plans   64
   questionnaires   65–66
   reports   56, 66–67
   safety   15–16
   schedules   49, 64
Auster, E. A.   19, 96, 102, 103, 104
Australia   12–13
autocratic management   80
automotive sector   10
Azzone, G.   85

barriers, organizational   77–92, 139–140, 147
beginner (organizations)   102
benchmarks   62
Bertelè, U.   85
Body Shop   8
Boeker, W.   111
Brent Spar   32
British Standards Institute   15
BS 5750 quality system   19
BS 7750   16, 19–20, 21, 22
BS 8555   22–23
budgets   72–75, 89

Business For Social Responsibility Education
   Fund   10
business integration   105–106
business objectives   71
business unit strategy   111

CAR (corrective action process)   51–52
Carson, Rachel   1
case studies   113–146
   devoid EMS   115–119, 120
   devolved EMS   125–134
   integrated EMS   137–146
   isolated EMS   120–124
certification   106, 114
change   17–18, 80–81
   case studies   133, 145
   communicating   85
   economic climates   147
   management   110
   organizational adaptation   109
Chernobyl, Soviet Union   3
classification, policies   98–99
clean technology   4
commitment
   management   26–27, 122, 126–127, 138, 144
   senior management   26, 81, 82–83, 87
communication   85–86
   case studies   118, 122–123, 132, 136,
      138–139, 142, 145
   informal   88
companies see organizations
Compaq/Hewlett Packard   90
competitive advantage   4, 8, 33–34
competitor discriminator   147–148
competitors   32, 33–34, 59–60
complexity   83, 88, 89, 122, 128, 143
compliance   17, 101
compliance-based attitude   87
compliance plus strategy   101
concerned citizen (organizations)   102
consumers   32, 33
continuous improvement   50, 62, 80
continuum models   96–97, 100–104
contractors   133

controls   25–26, 58, 90, 122, 123, 137
corporate environmentalism   4
corporate environmental plans *see* environmental
    management plans
corporate image   8, 9, 57
corporate performance   26, 62
corporate social responsibility   12–13
corrective action   51, 70
costs   1, 4, 73–74, 75
Council for the Protection of Rural England   33
creative context   100
credibility   4
credible plans   83, 118, 132
crisis preventive environmental management   99
critical nonconformities   70
culture   86–88, 110, 122, 142
customer measures   59
customers   9, 33, 85–86
customer tracking   61–62

data control   52–55
decision making   84, 88
deliberate proactive greening   98
deliberate reactive greening   97–98
democratic management   80
departmental analysis matrix   40–41
design   29, 30
design for the environment (DFE)   106–107
devoid EMS
    case study   115–119, 120
    model   114–115, 147
devolved EMS
    case studies   125–134
    model   125, 147
diminishing returns   74
direct costs   73–74, 75
directors
    case studies   117
    change   90–91
    environmental policy statements   27
    management commitment   26
    managing directors   48, 68, 71
    objectives   80–81
    see also senior management
distribution matrix   54
documents   52–55, 128, 131
Dorfman, M.   108–109
Dow Chemical   4, 5, 90
downsizing   125, 134, 145

Eco-Management and Audit Scheme (EMAS)
    16, 17, 20–21
eco-management audit   16–17, 20–21

economic development   4
economic downturns   115, 118, 140,
    144–145
economic policy   13
economic success   13–14
education   85
efficiency   1, 4, 6, 60
electronic data control   52, 55
EMAS (Eco-Management and Audit Scheme)
    16, 17, 20–21
emergent active greening   98
EMI Music   86
emission levels   59
employees
    change   85
    democratic management   80
    empowering   79
    encouragement   87
    innovation   84–85
    interviews   31
    involvement   44–45, 68
    morale   12–13, 57
    reports   57
    safety   80
    skills   31
    surveys   31
    training   87
EMS *see* environmental management systems
end-of-pipe technologies   84
energy   6, 7, 60
engineering   29, 30–31
environment, damage to   1
Environmental Act 1995:   42
environmental aspects   35
environmental assessment   31–32
environmental awareness   4, 14
environmental charters   11
environmental contexts   99–100
Environmental Data Services (ENDS)   11
environmental health and safety (EHS) systems
    135
environmental impacts   3, 35, 57, 59, 60
environmental improvements   13–14
environmentally friendly companies   4, 8, 33
environmental management   14, 30, 31
environmental management costs to sales ratios
    61
environmental management plans   14–15,
    70–72
    budget   72–75
    credible   83, 118, 132
    review   57–58
    targets   42–44

environmental management systems (EMS)
  accreditation 33
  aim 26
  benefits 91
  defined 15, 25
  development 15–23
  documentation 54–55
  history 17–19
  impact 26
environmental managers
  audits 49, 51, 56, 64
  CARs 51, 52
  case studies 116, 121, 130, 132
  distribution matrix 54
  environmental management plans 71
  larger companies 78
  management review 48, 49, 51
  nonconformities 46, 47–48
  role 14
environmental marketing 4
environmental performance 4
environmental performance indicators (EPI)
  58–60
environmental policy 11, 13, 26–27
environmental protection 4
Environmental Protection Act 1990: 41
environmental records 4
environmental risk 27, 59
  minimization 1, 3–5
environmental units 104–105
environmental working groups (EWG) 48, 68,
  71
Envirowise 14
EPI (environmental performance indicators)
  58–60
European Union (EU) 17
evaluation, management plans 61
evidence 66, 68
EWG (environmental working groups) 48, 68,
  71
excellence 101–102
expenses 74
external audits 28, 32–35
extraordinary management review meetings 70
Exxon Group 2

feedback 83
finance 28, 30, 60, 73
fire fighter (organizations) 102
five stage model 102–104
fluorescent tubes 7
focus groups 31
forecasts 34–35

Freisen, P. H. 81
Friends of the Earth 32
Fuller, M. K. 85

González-Benito, J. and O. 106
Greenhouse Challenge Plus 12–13
green image, companies 8, 9
greening model 97
green issues 4
Greenpeace 32
green wall 104–105
Greiner, L. E. 110

Hale, M. 25
Hart, S. 17
Haveman, M. 108–109
heating 7
Hillary, R. 91, 92
Hunt, C. B. 19, 96, 102, 103, 104
Hutchinson, C. 107

image, corporate 8, 9, 57
image-builders 85
incentives 90, 123, 128–129, 139
indirect costs 75
informal communication 88
information, flows 88
innovation 83–85
  attitude 87, 88
  case studies 118, 129, 134, 139,
    142–143
innovation-based green strategy 95
integrated EMS
  case studies 137–146
  model 135–136, 147
integrated systems see system integration
integrated technologies 84
internal audits 28–32, 55–56
investments 33
ISO 9000 series 22
ISO 9001: 19
ISO 14000: 9, 10, 22, 35
ISO 14001: 16, 20, 21–23
  accreditation 71
  audits 64
  case studies 116, 117, 121, 126, 141, 143
  certification 106
  consumers 33
  continuous improvement 51
  costs 75
  development 19, 26
  implementing 28
  operational transformation 105

isolated EMS
   case study   120–124
   model   119

jargon   71
job satisfaction   12

Khanna, M.   13
Kirkland, L. H.   6

larger organizations   77–78, 89
legislation   3, 11–12, 16
   companies unaware of   20
   environmental units   104
   growth of   32
   new   34
   organizational barriers   77
   register   41–42
lighting   7
litigation   4
local government   20
logical incrementalism   110–111
Lucent Technologies   10

management
   change   110
   commitment   26–27, 122, 126–127, 138,
      144
   procedures   45–56
   reports   57
   reviews   48–50, 63, 68–70
   style   79–81, 87, 126–127, 136
   traditional thinking   4, 109
   see also environmental management;
      managers; models; senior
      management
management approaches   87–88
management systems measures   59
managerial behaviour   81, 82
managers
   change   85, 90–91, 110
   functions   14
   innovation   84–85
   new strategies   89
   objectives   80–81
   training   85
   see also environmental managers; senior
      management
managing directors   48, 68, 71
market share   1
material nonconformities   46
measuring   57–62
media   32, 33

meetings
   management review   48, 49, 50, 68–70
   minutes   68–69
   plan review   58
Melton, K.   90
memo approach   31–32
middle managers see managers
Miller, D.   81
Mintzberg, H.   110, 111
minutes, management reviews   68–69
models   95–111, 113
   continuum   96–97, 100–104
   devoid EMS   114–115, 147
   devolved EMS   125, 147
   integrated EMS   135–136, 147
   isolated EMS   119
   typology   95–96, 97–98
monitoring   57–62
motivations   6

NCR (nonconformity reports)   47–48
noise   11
non-compliance strategy   101
nonconformities   45–48, 56, 65, 66, 70
nonconformity reports (NCR)   47–48
Northumbrian Water   10
nuclear incidents   2–3

objectives   42–44, 51, 62, 71–72
oil spills   2
operating procedures   45–56
operational practices   106
operational transformation   105–109, 123
opportunities   61
organizational theory   78
organizations
   barriers   77–92, 139–140, 147
   change see change
   drivers   5–13
   five stage model   102–104
   larger   77–78, 89
   profiles   113
   structure   90–91, 116, 131
   substructures   89
overheads   74

passive environmental strategy   94
Patel, P.   111
PDCA (Plan-Do-Check-Act) cycle   26, 107
Peircy, N.   90
personal contact   88
personnel   29, 30
Peters, T. J.   109

Pioneer Technology UK Ltd   8
Plan-Do-Check-Act (PDCA) cycle   26, 107
plans *see* environmental management plans
plant load factor (PLF)   60
POEM (product-oriented environmental
      management systems)   107–108
policies   98–99, 107–108, 109
pollution   11
Pollution Prevention Pays ('3Ps')   4, 5, 9
Porter, M. E.   83
pragmatist (organizations)   103
pre-environmental management system audits   28
pressure groups   32–33
preventive action   51, 70
proactive companies   95
proactive context   100
proactive environmental management   99
proactivist (organizations)   103–104
problem-solving resource   84–85
procedural nonconformities   46–47
procedures   45–56
process nonconformities   46
Producer Responsibility Legislation   8
production   1, 29, 30–31
product-oriented environmental management
      (POEM) systems   107–108
products   74, 84, 107
profiles, organizations   113
profitablity   1
profit and loss forecasts   73
Project Acorn   22–23
public interest   1
Punjari, D.   90

quality   17, 25
Quinn, J. B.   110

Ramus, C. A.   85, 95
reactive context   100
reactive environmental management   98–99
reactive environmental strategy   94
registers   36, 41–42
regulations   11, 104
Rennings, K.   84
research and development   29, 30
resources   45, 72–73
   available   89–90, 117
   case studies   117, 124, 127–128, 132–134,
      138, 142
resource usage measure   58–59
revenue   73–74
revision records   55
Roddick, Anita   8

Roome, N.   19, 101, 104
Rothenberg, S.   89
Royal Society for Nature Conservation   33

safety   15–16, 80
Sarabura, M.   90
SBU (strategic business units)   81, 89
SC Johnson   108–109
senior management   18, 19
   BS 7750   20
   case studies   116, 117, 126–127, 131
   commitment   26, 81, 82–83, 87
   communication   85
   environmental policy statements   27
   management reviews   56, 68
   new strategies   89, 90
   nonconformities   70
   see also directors; management; managers
Shell   32
Shelton, R. D.   18, 104–105, 109, 114
Shimell, P.   86
Shrivastava, P.   17
Silent Spring (Carson)   1
small to medium enterprises (SME)   91–92
stable context   100
staff *see* employees
stakeholders   26, 57
standards   16, 19–20, 21–23, 14000
   see also BS 5750; BS 7750; BS 8555; ISO;
      ISO 9000; ISO 14001; ISO 9001
Stone, L.   86
strategic attitude   87–88
strategic business units (SBU)   81, 89
strategic environmental management   99
strategic options model   101
strategies
   adoption   93, 110
   case studies   121
   complexity   89, 122, 128, 143
   effective   89
   implementation   111
   types   94–95
substructures, organizations   89
supervisors   85, 87
suppliers   9, 10, 23
Swanson, E. B.   85
system integration   88
   case studies   116–117, 122, 128, 131,
      137–138, 143–144
system nonconformities   47

Tapon, F.   90
targets   42–44, 51, 62, 71, 72

technology 4, 34, 84, 88–89
terminology 71
Tetra Pak 9
Thompson, D. 6
threats 61
Three Mile Island, USA 2
Tinsley, S. 90
Tokaimura, Japan 2
top management *see* senior management
Total Quality Environmental Management
     (TQEM) 16
Total Quality Management (TQM) 16
TQEM (Total Quality Environmental
     Management) 16
TQM (Total Quality Management) 16
trade-offs 109
traditional management thinking 4, 109
training 85, 87
typology models 95–96, 97–98

underperformance 61
unrealized greening 98

Valdez (ship) 2
Van der Linde, C. 83
Vastag, G. 88
Volvo 9

waste 6, 7–8, 12, 59
'Waste Reduction Always Pays' (WRAP) 4, 5,
     90
Waterman, R. H. 109
Winn, M. I. 97
working groups 48, 68
WRAP ('Waste Reduction Always Pays') 4, 5,
     90
Wright, G. 90

Younger, M. 111